Wake Up to Your Dreams

An Exploration of Dreams and Dreaming

Wake Up to Your Dreams

An Exploration of Dreams and Dreaming

Gilly Crow

Copyright © 2024 Gilly Crow

The moral right of the author has been asserted.

Cover design from an original artwork by Lorna and Stephen Kirin © 2021 (https://thekirins.com)
Copy Editor Kelly Derrick

Apart from any fair dealing for the purposes of research or private study, or criticism or review, as permitted under the Copyright, Designs and Patents Act 1988, this publication may only be reproduced, stored or transmitted, in any form or by any means, with the prior permission in writing of the publishers, or in the case of reprographic reproduction in accordance with the terms of licences issued by the Copyright Licensing Agency. Enquiries concerning reproduction outside those terms should be sent to the publishers.

Matador
Unit E2 Airfield Business Park,
Harrison Road, Market Harborough,
Leicestershire. LE16 7UL
Tel: 0116 2792299
Email: books@troubador.co.uk
Web: www.troubador.co.uk/matador
Twitter: @matadorbooks

ISBN 978 1805141 747

British Library Cataloguing in Publication Data.
A catalogue record for this book is available from the British Library.

Printed and bound in Great Britain by 4edge Limited
Typeset in 12pt Minion Pro by Troubador Publishing Ltd, Leicester, UK

Matador is an imprint of Troubador Publishing Ltd

For Jessica and Florence

CONTENTS

Acknowledgements		ix
Introduction		xi
Chapter 1	Stirring	1
Chapter 2	Waking Up	14
Chapter 3	Staying Awake	25
Chapter 4	The Invitation	35
Chapter 5	The Explorations	43
Finis		127
Postscript		129
Keeping a Dream Journal		132
Some Ideas for Working with Dreams		134
Glossary		144
Recommended Reading		148
References		151

ACKNOWLEDGEMENTS

I am wholly indebted to Dr Carl Jung, John O'Donohue and Roland Hindmarsh for their wisdom and guidance into the inner world of dreams and imagination. My gratitude goes to the Cambridge Jungian Circle for giving me the opportunity 'to pass into the Circle', to my family and all my dear friends for their love and support, and to all those over the years who have shared their dreams with me in openness and trust and have given permission for some of their dreams to be shared in this book. My heartfelt thanks to each and every member of the dream groups, who have journeyed and explored with me over the years with astonishing courage and offered such inspirational insights and encouragement in our mutual endeavours to wake up to our dreams.

> I imagine there are so many people woven into these words, each playing their part and each helping in their own way to bring this book to fruition.
> (Nicky, dream group member, 2021)

INTRODUCTION

If you are interested in working with your dreams "Wake up to your Dreams" is the book for you. It is accessible to all trainees and experienced practitioners as well as others who wish to look more deeply into their inner world.

By taking you through Jung's 'little hidden door' (Jung, 1964a: 304) the book encourages you into that inner world of unimaginable richness that, when acknowledged and explored, can bring about profound changes in your outer, waking life.

My hope in writing "Wake up to your Dreams" is that you will enjoy these adventures into our 'other world' and be inspired to open that 'hidden door' into the world of dreams where your life can be broadened and enriched beyond measure.

"Wake up to your Dreams" begins some 30 years ago with my introduction, as a newly qualified therapist working with my first client, to the then unexplored dream life of the unconscious. The book expands into how this initial awakening and interest in Jung blossomed into a series of my own extraordinary dreams that set me upon a path of never ending discovery that revealed the fascinating, puzzling and often unseen dimensions of alchemy and synchronicity. I share with you how these discoveries helped me to understand more of Jung's often challenging process of Individuation.

Individuation means trying to become the person we *really* are and not who we think or have been told we are or would like to be. This is not an easy road to travel but the journey is worth every step you take even if, like me, you only catch an occasional glimpse of the destination.

"Wake up to your Dreams" shows you, through my own experience, how easy it is to resist this process, an example is vividly described in a dream about the writing of this book. However much we resist, the unconscious will constantly and seemingly inexorably, continue to beckon us through our dreams to live a more authentic life.

From my personal discoveries, insights and inspirations the book then moves into the expansion of the dreamwork in my one to one work as an integrative psychotherapist, strongly influenced by Carl Jung, to the formation, in 2011, of three ongoing dream groups. "Wake up to your Dreams" gives you a glimpse into the work we do collaboratively over a whole day and demonstrates how dynamic, demanding but incredibly rewarding dreamwork in a group can be.

In the chapter, The Explorations, you will find authentic examples of group members' and clients' dreams, how they were worked with and in several the outcomes, sooner or later, of the dreamwork that led to lasting change for the dreamer.

The dreams have been chosen to represent a wide range of different 'types' of dream and cover prognostic, warning, recurring/repeating, waking, the shadow, linked dreams, collective and one that does not fit into any category.

The creation of a safe and held space to explore dreams is emphasised throughout the book. You are encouraged to find a trusted, experienced guide who can help you to develop your imagination and intuition in dreamwork while ensuring the ground under your feet remains stable as we do need to transition comfortably and safely between our inner and outer worlds.

Introduction

The book concludes with an 'ending' dream of mine that is left open for you to explore.

To help you in your explorations of the dream world you will find at the end of book notes of how to keep a dream journal, some ideas for working with dreams, a glossary of the Jungian terms used, a recommended further reading list and references to the quotes used in the book.

Gilly Crow Bsc.Hons
MBACP Reg. Senior Accredited Psychotherapist
Senior Accredited Supervisor
May 2022

We live between the act of awakening and the act of surrender.
Each morning we awaken to the light and the invitation to a new
day in the world of time;
each night we surrender to the dark
to be taken to play in the world of dreams where time is no more.
(O'Donohue, 2004: 11)

1

Stirring

> I bless the night that nourished my heart
> To set the ghosts of longing free
> Into the flow and figure of dream that went to harvest from the dark
> Bread for the hunger no one sees.
> (O'Donohue, 2007: 27)

How did dreams become such an important part of my life and the work I do as a psychotherapist? How was it that the messages of 'it's only your imagination' and 'thank goodness it was only a dream' changed to a realisation that it was these very experiences that help us to gain access to an understanding of our dreamworld – a world that holds a key to our inner and outer well-being?

Some 30 years ago, towards the end of my second year of training, I began work with my very first client. She presented with general feelings of anxiety, occasional panic attacks, difficulty in getting off to sleep and several physical ailments. Despite her intensely traumatic story she appeared to show little affect in relating it. She sat calm and composed, revealing a life beset by difficulty, tragedy, trauma, illness and guilt, but it was as if she was not involved and these events had happened and were happening to someone else. Then, at the end of our fourth session, she said suddenly, 'I'm having all these dreams. I wake up four or five times a night from a disturbing dream. It's almost as if I'm living another life while I'm asleep. I don't know whether dreams have any significance?'

I had no experience in working with dreams, but I was intrigued as at the end of each session I would feel overwhelmed, intensely sad and sometimes very angry, recognising that I was in a strong countertransference and puzzling as to where *her* emotional and inner connection with her story might be. Could it possibly be in those nightly excursions into the dreamworld?

I took these first bewildering experiences to my weekly supervision with a very experienced Jungian psychotherapist.

During my psychodynamic training I had been drawn to Jung in a way that is difficult to explain. Intellectually, I would often be at a loss to understand him and struggled to make sense of his writing. But somehow his words resonated with me, as if I recognised, understood and absorbed them in my heart.

It was therefore important to me that my supervisor was a Jungian (a word that Jung heartily disliked!), so that I could learn more about Jung's ways of working, particularly with the unconscious. It was equally important that my supervisor was male, as I had been brought up in an almost entirely female family, with the men in my life often absent from home. I had attended an all-girls' school and had two daughters. I needed the balance of a 'male' way of thinking. After my first supervisor retired, all of my supervisors, until recently, have been male Jungian analysts from whom I have learned the inestimable value of working deeply, creatively and, above all, relationally with my clients. Although Jung's theories resonate deeply with me, Jung himself placed much greater emphasis on the quality of the therapeutic or supervisory relationship.

> It is in fact largely immaterial what sort of technique [the therapist] uses, for the point is not the technique but the person who uses it. (Jung, 1964c:159)

On presentation to my supervisor of the difficulties I was experiencing with the client, he leaned forward and in his gentle way suggested that I asked her to share one of her dreams with me.

And, astonishingly, there it was, being played out almost every night in her nightmarish dreamworld where all the traumas of the past were being vividly re-enacted, albeit in the disguised language and images of the unconscious. The feelings were too powerful to be experienced in the client's waking life, so they had been dissociated from and split off into the shadow world of dreams. From my supervisor I very gradually learned how to stay with and work safely within this shadow world.

The client was remembering three or four vivid dreams a night and my weekly supervision became the Jungian training ground for adventuring – with my supervisor as an experienced guide – into the dreamworld of my client. Dreamwork slowly began to form the foundation of my developing therapeutic work.

Dreams are a universal and seemingly essential experience and ongoing research suggests that lack of rapid-eye movement (REM) sleep deprives us of the dreaming phase of sleep, which can lead to health problems (Carr, 2017).

I would ask the client to choose one dream to work on and write the rest down in a dream journal (see p. 132), which would go some way towards containing them and bringing them further into consciousness. By working carefully with images, associated feelings and their echoes with the past, we slowly brought the chosen dream into a greater awareness of its connection to her waking difficulties.

But how did she 'choose'? Outwardly the choice seemed to be a rational, even intellectual decision, but we gradually realised that the choice appeared to be based on some kind of unconscious processing. The client would frequently describe a current traumatic event that she assumed to be the sole cause of her distress, only to discover that underneath this event her 'chosen' dream revealed the deeper, hidden issues of the past that had been triggered by the experience in her waking life and were being brought to her attention.

We learned how helpful it could be to look at this trigger and the context surrounding the dream in her daily personal life, so that her conscious experience could be further illuminated by the information being made available by her unconscious through the dream.

After many months of therapy and dreamwork the client eventually began to bring about a healing of old 'heart wounds', releasing anger, grief and guilt and finding some relief from the traumatic memories she held in her body. Slowly she began to develop a more rounded and robust sense of her true self.

In Jung's *Modern Man in Search of a Soul* I found the corroboration for my experience with this client. He says:

> Dreams give information about the secrets of the inner life and reveal to the dreamer hidden factors of his personality. As long as these are undiscovered, they disturb his waking life and betray themselves only in the form of symptoms ... there must be a thorough-going conscious assimilation of unconscious contents.
> (Jung, 1985: 18)

This client and the supervision I received were priceless gifts, opening a door to a growing understanding of a whole other dimension of 'reality' that resides within us, if only we can find the courage to cross the threshold from the known to the unknown world.

The question I ask myself is, what was at work beneath our conscious awareness that brought this first client to me? She had no waking realisation that she brought me a gift that was to form the backbone of my therapeutic work, and I held no prior knowledge that this was to be so.

Had I unconsciously chosen to follow this path and my client had somehow picked up that she had a part to play in this? Could this be a manifestation of Jung's 'collective unconscious' – that sea of possibilities in which we are all baptised and where we are all connected in unfathomable ways?

The path before me began to open up in the early 1990s. At a time of personal crisis, I experienced a series of dreams that are as vivid to me today as they were then and that showed me clearly the direction I was being invited to take.

The first dream – The Golden Stone – was unlike any other I had experienced before.

The Golden Stone

> *One night, while deeply asleep yet curiously 'awake', I heard a voice, wonderfully whole and resonant and, I think, male, speaking to me. It said, 'The truth is in the golden stone, wake up and write it down.'*
>
> *My immediate response in the dream was to say, 'But I'm fast asleep and I don't want to wake up and write it down.'*

Throughout the night the voice would speak again and again with the same message, until wearily at 5 a.m., I finally consented to wake up and write it down. I felt immediate relief.

Jung says:

> The dream represents a situation equivalent to reality ... a kind of wakened state ... the unconscious seems bent on conveying a powerful impression of reality to the dreamer, an impression which is emphasised by *repetition*.
> (Jung, 1983: 257, my emphasis)

> The voice has as a rule an absolutely authoritative character and generally comes *at decisive moments*.
> (Jung, 1989a: 196, my emphasis)

But what on earth was the golden stone and how could the truth be in it? There had been no figure in the dream, no colour, action, no actual stone, no images at all, simply the voice. I felt the dream was giving me an answer to something I had long sought, if only I could understand it.

During a meditation on the morning before the dream, the words 'research the Centre' had come into my mind, and it seemed not improbable that the meditation and the dream were linked. The dream seemed starkly simple yet profoundly complicated. Asleep, I had been extremely resistant to doing what I was asked, but awake I could not get it out of my mind.

As the day after the dream wore on, I kept finding myself in the study. A very recently purchased, *unopened* book – *An Illustrated Encyclopaedia of Symbols*, by J. C Cooper (1978) – lay on the table. I opened it.

Under 'stone' there were many references, but one group held my attention. Among alchemical meanings were the 'philosopher's stone', 'supreme quest', 'reconciliation of all opposites', 'attainment of unity' and *'regaining the Centre'*. Somehow, these meanings resonated deeply within me.

The references to gold, keeping again to alchemical meanings, included 'essence of the sun', 'turning base metal into gold is transmutation of the soul', 'regaining the primordial purity of human nature' and *'attaining the Centre'*.

You can probably imagine how carried away I was with the first part of the dream – it was dramatic and special (therefore I must be special). So engrossed was I by the first part of the dream that it took, I am ashamed to say, a whole year for the equally, if not more important, second part of the dream – 'wake up and write it down' – to even register.

And how had I responded? 'I'm fast asleep and I don't want to wake up and write it down!' What I appeared to be actually saying was: 'I am relatively unconscious and have no interest in waking up my consciousness and becoming more self-aware.'

How easily I had fallen into hubris by 'hearing' what I unconsciously wanted to hear and led myself away from the much more difficult task of understanding what waking up and writing it down really meant. To have looked only at my initial response to the voice would have created disequilibrium within myself, the very imbalance and ambivalence I needed to work on.

Writing it down – whatever 'it' is – is something I have long been resistant to. Another dream some 20 years later helped me to understand that resistance – the dream of the cow/bull (see p. 15) – and here I am, 30 years after The Golden Stone dream, at last trying to 'write it down'!

Many years later I can see that, at the time, I experienced The Golden Stone dream only as personal to me, but now it has a feeling of also being collective, a meaningful message to us all that I was fortunate enough to pick up.

The 'waking up' was enormously encouraged and helped by joining, in 1992, the newly formed Cambridge Jungian Circle (CJC). Just prior to this the same voice had spoken to me again one night with the words, 'You must pass into the Circle'. So it seemed there was to be no escape.

At the inaugural meeting of the CJC, small groups were formed to study particular aspects of Jung's work. I made a beeline for the alchemy and individuation group and there, over the course of some 13 years, I found a resonance with my own inner journey and a guide to lead me through life, which is still an ongoing process. Alchemy and dreamwork appear to be so closely interwoven that the study of one enhances and illuminates the other.

As my journey progressed, two further dreams encouraged me to continue on the path before me. In the first:

I find myself standing on lush green grass looking down into a beautiful clear pool some feet below me. There are myriad small, smooth stones covering the bed of the pool. I notice a male figure, dressed in a blue robe, walking towards me and the voice speaks again saying, 'This is Jung's pool'. I do not know whether it is the figure who speaks. There is a feeling of absolute peace as I stand there.

The second arrived shortly after this:

I am standing opposite Dr Jung in his study at Küsnacht. He is dressed in a tweed suit and leans towards me smiling and with a twinkle in his eye. He speaks to me.

On waking, try as I might I could not, and still cannot, recall what he said. Perhaps one day when I am ready to hear it will come back to me.

So, dreams can be life changing, offering both challenge and comfort as we struggle to become more of who we really are, as in Jung's process of Individuation. This is not a linear progression but circular and spiral, described by Jung (1953) as a circumambulation around the Centre or Self.

We come in and out at different points, endlessly repeating processes, sometimes consciously and at other times unconsciously, until we occasionally get a sense of something solid forming within us. This is the beginning of a consolidation to form that Centre or Self – the Philosopher's Stone or, as was once beautifully described to me, the 'jewel in the heart of the being'.

Just a note of 'encouragement' here. As I understand it, Individuation is a never-ending process of discovery about oneself and is classically not about the destination but the journey and adventure to try and get there, as very few people actually arrive. I certainly have not, as the attainment of the supreme quest of becoming wholly who we are born to be, a task of seemingly unimaginable magnitude, still appears an impossibly long way off.

As my practice developed, I found myself again and again in what seemed like a foreign country, but I found Jung offered me a map of the territory, a grasp of the language and an insight into symbolic meaning.

In the course of my 'stirring' I began to experience an increase in synchronistic events. They had of course been there all along, waiting to be noticed, but I had not recognised them.

I remember a client in a midlife crisis who had been struggling to let go of a damaging relationship. One day she came into the room as usual, through the French windows, carefully shutting them behind her. She sat down and said with a triumphant smile, 'I've done it, I've finally shut the door on him'. At this precise moment one of the French windows slowly opened, showing us that part of her still had the door open to this relationship!

Synchronicities continue to inform my practice and my own adventures into the inner world, affirming for me that nothing is separate, that psyche and matter are irrevocably knit together in a wonderful whole, each being a part of the other.

For me this is the alchemical 'as above so below', a quote attributed to Hermes Trismegistus in *The Emerald Tablet* (the original source of *The Tablet* is unclear); or 'as within so without', where our external world is a reflection of our internal world, so that actively engaging with our dreams and inner process can bring about change in our outer experience.

How easy it is to look for answers in the fragile, outer material world instead of the much more difficult task of seeking where the answer really lies – within our inner being, which, unlike the material world, is eternal and indestructible.

Jung finds the words to affirm this:

> Even if the whole world were to fall to pieces, the unity of the psyche could never be shattered. And the wider and more numerous the fissures on the surface, the more this unity is strengthened in the depths.
> (Jung, 1964b: 305)

The 'midlife crisis' seemed to present itself to me more often than anything else. As I was also in midlife, I was reminded again and again to work in therapy on my own changing perception of myself and to experience both within myself and with my clients the struggle of the Self to make itself known through what we can experience as the 'dark gifts' of illness, tragedy, depression, disappointed hopes, redundancy, bereavement and, of course, in dreams.

However, as we explore the less familiar aspects of ourselves, the conscious mind often makes desperate attempts to cling to what is known, established and apparently 'safe', but that in reality is a destructive holding on to old patterns and belief systems that produce little but unhappiness in both mind and body. But, in the inner world of dreams, it is my understanding that the psyche strives constantly to reveal our inner truth, and if we ignore the messages of our dreamworld our bodies will often manifest the imbalances through illness and accident.

Almost daily I experience the relevance Jung has to me, and in the work I do it is borne out by the clients who have never heard of him yet share experiences of the psyche that match Jung's conclusions of what it means to be a human being.

Dream Musings

Dreams can be like the ocean. Sometimes they crash noisily like stormy waves on to the shore of our sleeping selves and wake us up. At other times they approach gently, almost silently, edging us slowly towards consciousness and, just as they land on the shore of our awakening, the pull of the tide urges the ocean back into itself. Try as we might to run into the water to touch that particular wave, we cannot find it among the mighty swell of the ocean.

The crashing dreams are often more easily remembered, especially if we can quickly repeat them to ourselves or write them down (see 'Keeping a Dream Journal', p. 132) but many of our dreams slip silently and tantalisingly back into the ocean.

Writing down our immediate feeling can help and sometimes, during the waking hours that follow, we may suddenly be prompted to remember an image, an interaction, a feeling. Unconsciously we may pick up a word or image from the newspaper, the TV, a conversation or see an object that has a similarity to a dream object prompting us to consciously remember more of the 'forgotten' dream.

Sometimes 'high dream phases' occur at or before times of important change in our lives. The big dreams, carrying a significant message, often appear during these phases. I have also noticed how frequently meaningful dreams seem to be influenced by the full moon!

There are several different types of dreams that appear more regularly in our nightly visits to the dreamworld. They include *retrospective dreams*, which may show us experiences from the past that we need to learn from; *sorting dreams*, which appear to go through and possibly rearrange the events of the previous day to bring about greater insight; *recurring dreams*, which help us to recognise long-held, unresolved issues; *nightmares*, which can bring to our attention an urgent need to confront a perceived threat to our outer or inner world; and *prognostic dreams*, which seem to show us events that have not yet happened, either to ourselves or others, but turn out to be true (see, for example, Nigel Hamilton's book, *Awakening Through Dreams* (2014)).

Not every dream can or needs to be categorised, they simply arrive for a purpose that may not be understood at the time, or indeed ever (see Sarah's dream, p. 122). Dreamtime is not the same as waking, clock time. It has its own rhythm and pace in bringing to our attention all that our inner world is trying to share with us and how that affects our waking life.

Dreams are also masters of disguise and displacement, often using symbols to represent both our waking life and unconscious experiences and their language can be very different from our waking world. Dreams often communicate in non-rational, seemingly obscure and what can appear at times to be befuddling nonsense, as vividly described by Jung:

> The dream is often occupied with apparently very silly details, thus producing an impression of absurdity ... But when at last we penetrate to its real meaning ... we discover that an apparently quite senseless dream is in the highest degree significant and that in reality it speaks only of important and serious matters.
> (Jung, [1972] 1990: 24)

Far more is going on in our unknown, unconscious world than in our conscious, waking world. Jung realised that something natural was at work within us that could bridge that seemingly impossible divide between those worlds – the transcendent function (Jung, [1972] 1990: 80).

Through dreams, active imagination (Chodorow, 1997) and in-depth therapy, the transcendent function allows unconscious contents to be brought nearer to consciousness so that the holding of the opposites between the 'imaginary' and 'real' world can be sustained and eventually united in a coming together, known to the alchemists as the *Coniunctio*, to form the Philosopher's Stone or Self. This is an ongoing, lifetime process.

'Take off your head' is an oft-used phrase in our dreamwork. This can feel extremely threatening for some people, whose psychological safety is invested only in what they perceive as the facts of the 'real' world, and their defence needs to be respected. But, in order to get a glimpse of what our dreamworld is trying to show us, we do need to put our logical, intellectual, rational mind to one side and embrace our intuition, creativity and, above all, our imagination.

Often perceived as anathema by more rational minds,

imagination was experienced very differently by the old alchemists, those keepers of the ancient wisdom.

Martin Ruland, a late Middle Ages and early Renaissance alchemist, stated that 'imagination is the star in man, the celestial or super celestial body' (Ruland quoted in Jung, 1989a: 277), and shows us that imagination was held in the highest esteem and not dismissed as irrational nonsense – a strong introjected message that many of us carry throughout our lives and can form part of our defences against the inner world.

If we can maintain the courage to follow our imagination, then we will find the hidden treasures of our own inner wisdom waiting for us to discover them.

Waking up to our dreams can, as I have discovered, be a life-changing, inspiring experience. Dreams hold the truth of ourselves and our experiences if only we can be open and patient enough to wait for the dream wisdom to unfold in our lives.

2

Waking Up

Each person is always on the threshold between their inner world and their outer world, between light and darkness, between known and unknown, between question and quest, between fact and possibility. This threshold runs through every experience we have, and our only real guide to this world is the imagination.

(O'Donohue, 2015: 21)

In the summer of 2010 an unexpected opportunity for that wisdom to unfold was presented to me. I was offered the chance to study, in one year, for an honours degree, something that had not been available when I undertook my initial three-year training. Although that training had then been supplemented by several courses including gestalt, transpersonal psychology and analytical psychology, plus three different trainings in supervision and senior accreditations both as a psychotherapist and supervisor, I still felt something was missing, as if I had not achieved some latent potential.

With a mixture of excitement and trepidation I prepared to set forth on this next stage, determined to enjoy everything it offered. It felt as if a new threshold was opening up before me – one that I needed to cross …

Then, on 18th October 2010, shortly after starting the course, I had the 'waking-up' dream that follows.

Dream of the Cow/Bull

Context

Having left school some 50 years ago I was somewhat out of touch with composing an academic essay, so I attended an optional day's essay-writing course run by the training organisation on 17th October.

Dream

My cousin meets me on holiday in a cottage, she is moving house but never asks me to visit. Then we are on a train as third-class passengers. My cousin is getting changed. The train goes no further and stops in a siding at some distance from the platform. I somehow get out and hold my right arm and hand out to people of all varieties to help them jump across the gap.

Then I'm on a walk in a very large, park-like space, my cousin is no longer present. At a distance I see a party of schoolchildren also on a walk. It is a lovely day and I stand by a gate into a small field that contains a very heavily built, extremely large and distinctively marked black and white cow/bull. The rest of the herd (normal Friesians) are in an adjacent field.

I see several riderless horses coming up a long avenue to my left and a man with a black dog and two small boys aged 8–10 years of age, ambling about behind the horses.

Suddenly the cow/bull breaks out of the field and charges down the avenue towards them. The man lets the dog off the lead and it escapes into an adjacent field. The cow/bull chases the man and boys up the avenue towards me. Then, just opposite me, the man and older boy escape through the barbed wire fence, but the younger boy gets caught on the fence and the cow/bull attacks him. The child screams. He is caught between the cow/bull's front legs, but with great difficulty the father manages to pull the boy free.

Next, almost instantaneously, the cow/bull is saddled and bridled, with one or both of the boys in front and father behind. But the reins are dangling down in front of the animal's front legs. I think this is potentially dangerous. The father shouts at one of the boys to gather up the reins over the cow/bull's head. He does so and the cow/bull becomes entirely docile. I am amazed.

Dreamwork

Insights into this dream arrived a few days later, shortly after a therapy session where the dream was looked at without much apparent success. I was in the *kitchen* possibly cooking or clearing up when the insights arrived. The kitchen is alchemically a place of transformation.

Clarification and Amplification

I am in the dream but, apart from the first part, only observing.

How old? Mid/late forties when I started counselling training.

Clothes: Unclear, but summery. I appear to be suitably 'dressed' for this experience?

Setting: Settings are unknown – I am in an unfamiliar place in my inner world. I am initially inside at the cottage and on the train, which are both in rural settings possibly indicating an internal, more unconscious but organic process taking place? Outside in the park I feel more at home, so perhaps a more conscious process towards outer life taking place in a natural setting?

Time of year and day: Summer, very bright, a beautiful, clear, warm day. An indication that the internal/external 'weather' is 'set fair' for this experience. Roughly midday, showing this was contemporary with my actual age (middle age) when I first started counselling training, so something that is connected to that learning experience?

The cottage: my time off is usually spent in a holiday cottage. In the dream the holiday is over, possibly showing me that the time has come for the real work to begin.

My cousin: I recognise my cousin but probably as a not very distinct (perhaps more unconscious) aspect of me that used to lead a rather sad, unfulfilled life and did not achieve full potential. In the dream I am relating to her actions and choices in a neutral way.

This cousin part has been taking a holiday but is then moving house altogether and does not want me to join her, so am I now to leave this part behind – sideline it?

We have travelled a short distance together (our lives so far), but have put ourselves in third class, perhaps symbolising the cousin part's belief that her intellect/ability/potential is only third class? The cousin aspect changes and I seem to have no need/desire to travel further with her. She is moving away and I am not invited to visit her. She will not participate in the course.

The train: is old-fashioned, possibly a steam train, compartments, pull-up/-down windows with leather straps, the sort of train we travelled on as a family when off on holiday. I *have* to get off this train, it goes no further and has come to the end of its journey. Might this train represent out-dated ancestral patterns and unconscious belief systems that 'a woman's place is in the home' not at university?

I must take a leap of faith to get off this train, as the gap between the train and the solid platform is quite wide. This takes effort and courage.

The gap: could be the gap between my conscious and unconscious and my old and potential new life. It's quite wide but I can get across it. I do not have to be stuck on the train.

The platform: might be the realisation that I now have the opportunity to change aspects of my life. Perhaps a 'platform' for the real work has been provided?

My right arm/hand: I am right-handed, right is generally more conscious, but it could also be showing me this is the *right, not wrong,* way forward.

The unknown people: about 15 of them. They are of every colour, creed, age and gender. They could be the panoply of unconscious shadow figures; *unlived* parts of myself that I need to integrate to participate fully in this next stage of my life.

> Perhaps your unlived lives run parallel to your current life and in some subtle way continue to influence the choices you make. All this might be happening beside you and in you, yet unknown to you. Maybe these unlived yet still unfolding lives are the sustenance from which your chosen life draws.
> (O'Donohue, 2007: 223)

(I ask myself if it might be possible that those unlived lives sometimes appear in our dreams?)

In this part of the dream I am actively engaged, perhaps indicating a more conscious involvement with the inner process.

In the second, very different, part of the dream I am almost completely passive, showing that the content is relatively unconscious and not being engaged with.

The walk in the park: it seems as though I have thought of the course as 'a walk in the park', something that I could undertake easily without too much effort or stress!

The dream then *compensates* for this attitude. The course could actually be extremely challenging.

The party of schoolchildren: they are all girls in uniform, 10 or 11 years old, walking in a crocodile with a teacher, very reminiscent of my grammar school days. This shows me there is a somewhat distant realisation that the course is an academic and learning environment, something I had left behind over 50 years ago.

The gate: there is a gateway/threshold to greater understanding in front of me.

The small field: the container is too small for its contents.

The cow/bull: the most powerful image in the dream. Its most striking aspect is its size, build, distinctive black and white colour and that it appears to be androgynous. This could suggest that it contains both feminine and masculine aspects of me. It holds the opposites. It is definitely a Friesian, possibly a pun on something frozen within but with the potential to provide life and essential nourishment?

Black and white: the cow/bull could constellate my greatest fear of writing (usually presented as black and white) in a required academic format, where I can be judged and found wanting and not what I seem to be.

Do I hold an introjected belief system that there is only *one* acceptable way – the academic – to communicate on paper? The cow/bull appears to be safely *penned up*, perhaps a pun on my belief that to keep it safe from criticism my writing cannot be imaginative, free flowing and truly expressed. And which part of me imprisoned it?

The cow/bull is *enormous*, possibly showing me that the fear of writing is *out of all proportion* and separated from other more integrated parts of me, the herd of Friesians, quietly grazing together untroubled by the cow/bull.

The riderless horses: appear from my left – approaching out of the unconscious – but it is an *uphill* journey to get to me. In the dream I know they are not mares (pun, not a nightmare?), but I'm unsure if they are stallions or geldings. They are wild and free, possibly symbolising the intellectual freedom of the masculine aspect of me and they have no fear of the cow/bull.

They could also be a metaphor for either 'wild horses *will not* drag this out of me' or conversely that 'wild horses are coming *to* drag this out of me'.

The man and two boys: again, approaching uphill from the unconscious. They could all be animus figures at varying stages of development. There is the responsible, mature masculine aspect that can embody spirit, reason, intellect and the light of consciousness and the boys could be younger, less developed or regressed aspects of me.

Their ages correspond to primary school and passing the 11+ examination. At this stage, perhaps I felt I could not fulfil the unspoken parental expectations of success so some 'unwelcome' creative aspects of me retreated into the shadow?

The black dog: this could be a shadow, unlived, depressed aspect of me, symbolising my suppressed, imaginative creativity. In the dream I do not *recognise* the dog – do not recognise my instinctive but depressed abilities? The mature animus figure has this confined on a lead but when threatened by the cow/bull lets it off so that it can escape and run freely to safety, perhaps showing that if I can trust and let go then I *can* express myself freely without fear.

The avenue: the Judy Garland and Fred Astaire song 'A Couple of Swells' immediately comes to mind. They have an invitation but cannot find any means of getting to their destination and decide:

> So we'll walk up the Avenue
> Yes, we'll walk up the Avenue
> Yes, a walk up the Avenue's what we'll take.

This could be showing me that there is only one way to 'get there' and that is to accept the 'invitation' being offered, while understanding that to arrive at my destination I must use my own metaphorical two feet!

The charging of the cow/bull: the fear suddenly and without warning breaks out and charges downhill (towards the unconscious) and the animus figures.

This could be the part of me that is finding it hard to let go of the fear of writing so, *as a protective but negative aspect of the Self* (Kalsched, 1996) it tries to disable the animus figures, symbolising thought and spirit, that could disempower the fear and render it redundant. The negative protective Self that I have created would find this possibility extremely threatening, as it would seem to put me in a psychologically very unsafe place.

The charging cow/bull could also be a symbol of my unconscious *rage* at *having* to write academic dissertations subject to the judgement of others.

The animus figures are, however, driven towards me by the cow/bull, but I do nothing to help them and simply observe the scene. I am still detached from these masculine parts of Self?

Becoming the charging cow/bull: at this point in the dreamwork I felt drawn towards engaging more fully with the cow/bull, so I allowed myself to drop into the image. This is what happened:

> *I am pawing the ground, blowing noisily through my nostrils. I feel huge, immensely powerful and full of rage. The pen is too small and I have an overwhelming urge to break out. Part of me wants to have more space like the rest of the herd, but also to be free like the wild horses. It is a wonderful feeling as I charge out and thunder down the hill, terrifying everything in my path. But another part needs to chase those intruding animus figures up to the pen and confine them so they are imprisoned and I can maintain the inner status quo, but this is an uphill, ambivalent struggle and I do not succeed.*

Experiencing the cow/bull helped me to understand just how powerfully it had influenced my unconscious fear of academic writing and the rage I felt towards this perceived limitation of my creativity.

The escape of the animus figures: my more mature animus and the slightly older boy are able to escape from the fear and possible imprisonment, but the younger one gets caught 'on the fence', gets hurt and is unsure if he can escape the cow/bull? At age 8 was I caught 'on the fence' about something?

My almost unknown father returned from the war in 1945 and shortly after my very authoritarian grandmother moved in with us. Perhaps this young, previously free-spirited, masculine aspect of me suddenly had to conform to being controlled by a more rigid way of life?

In trying to metaphorically escape from this, the young emerging animus is trapped in a painful place – the barbed wire designed to 'keep in' potentially 'unruly' parts of Self. It is a struggle for the 'father' animus figure to free the boy and release him from his fear?

As soon as the younger part is freed the fear can be brought under control.

The saddling and bridling of the cow/bull: the two younger animus figures sit at the front with the 'father' animus figure behind. The dream shows that the cow/bull can be 'tamed' sufficiently to allow the safe written expression of my imagination?

The reins: are dangling down in front of the animal's legs. This could be an indication that unless the cow/bull *is* metaphorically 'reined in' I will have no authority over the 'beast' that lies within.

At this point I seem to have the only *thought* in the dream that *this is a potentially dangerous situation*, indicating that, if the fear is not to go on the rampage again, I need guidance from the animus to bring it under control.

The father has to make himself heard *urgently* in case the cow/bull charges off again. He shouts to the boy to gather up the reins over the cow/bull's *head* – the intellect has to be 'tamed' by the youngest wounded animus figure, but there is a danger he will not listen?

Once this is done the cow/bull becomes entirely docile – *the fear has been 'reined in'*?

Strongest feelings: first, the horror when the youngest boy is caught on the fence and is being attacked and the relief when the fear is 'reined in'. Second, the utter amazement that this has been accomplished relatively easily.

The dream was worked through mostly on my own over a period of time, and now when I read it through again fresh insights still arrive, underlining Jung's statement:

> I do not understand my own dreams any better than any of you, for they are always somewhat beyond my grasp and I have the same trouble with them as anyone who knows nothing about dream interpretation. Knowledge is no advantage where it is a matter of one's own dreams.
> (Jung, [1935] 1977: 122)

Outcome: I went on to complete my degree just in time to celebrate my seventieth birthday.

In the journalling, *unmarked* aspect of the course the writing flowed easily. In the academic, *marked* written work the cow/bull part of me often became either 'penned up' with fear or rampaged wildly at the perceived limitation of my imagination.

I repeatedly found myself metaphorically caught on the barbed wire, but the dream helped me to understand that this need not be a permanent situation and that I did have the inner resources to free myself.

I was quite surprised to discover that at the end of the course I had absolutely no inclination to attend the degree ceremony with the obligatory photograph of myself in the external trappings of cap and gown.

Instead, what mattered was the experience of moving inwardly from the known to the unknown, from possibility to fact and the undertaking of the quest.

But, above all, it was the wonderful lifelong friends I made, who, in asking that I run a dream group for them, helped me across the threshold from fear to courage, to move from question to quest and to continue, with their encouragement and companionship, my exploration into dreams.

3

Staying Awake

The Dream Groups

> Had I the heavens' embroidered cloths,
> Enwrought with gold and silver light,
> The blue and the dim and the dark cloths
> Of night and light and the half-light,
> I would spread the cloths under your feet,
> But I, being poor, have only my dreams,
> I have spread my dreams under your feet,
> Tread softly because you tread on my dreams.
> *(Yeats, 1994: 90)*

The dreamwork had slowly begun to form the backbone to the skeleton of my deepening understanding of the therapeutic process. As the skeleton fleshed out and took on life and energy, opportunities to widen my experience with dreamwork presented themselves.

Without any conscious invitation on my part, two other groups of psychotherapists approached me, asking if I could run a dream group for them. The first started in 2011, the second quickly followed and the third shortly after that. All the groups are still running at my home, meeting together for a whole day. Each group has developed in its own way, but all offer mutual support and encouragement to engage with the inner world and from that to live a more authentic life.

It is part of our contract that whatever happens during the day is confidential and, although we are all active psychotherapists, that we do not become the therapist to other members of the group. Our explorations into the dreamworld aim to be collaborative, respectful, co-creative and sensitive.

An important part of the group process is to allow each person the opportunity to share where they are at the beginning of the day and where they have arrived at the end of the day. We intuitively choose an angel card[1] in the morning and a dragon card[2] as we finish. We are frequently astonished by how accurately the cards reflect the dreams we have shared and our inner and outer lives at that moment in time.

In the groups, although we use many of the ideas included in 'Some Ideas for Working with Dreams' at the end of this book (see p. 134), we do not adhere to them too rigidly. Apart from following the *sequence* of the dream, being aware of someone drifting into extraneous connections and looking for echoes in the dreamer's waking life, we are mostly guided by our spontaneous and intuitive responses.

During the dreamwork we explore the dreams rather than excavate them to the point where they become an intellectual reductive exercise that takes us away from the feelings, actions, insights and numinosity of the dreams. This is not easy to replicate in the written word.

The dreamer is asked to share the dream in the *present tense* as this brings the dream more alive and also encourages 'forgotten' elements to be remembered. *There is no interruption from the group*

---

1 The Original Angel Cards, WorldTree Press, https://worldtreepress.com
2 Dragon Cards, www.oneheartweb.com

during the telling. At the end of the dreamwork we *always* check out how the dreamer is feeling and often have a good shake to free our bodies from anything unwanted that we may have unconsciously absorbed somatically during the work.

The group is together for a good six hours at each meeting and, although we do endeavour to leave the dreamwork in a safe place, much of our dreamwork remains incomplete at the time, awaiting further illumination from our subsequent night adventures into the dreamworld. All group members have access to additional support outside the group.

Over the years in groups and one to one I have noticed that when a recurring dream (sometimes of many years standing) is explored for the first time *it never recurs in that form to the dreamer.* This was also Jung's experience as, after finally understanding a persistent recurring dream, he states: 'I never had the dream again' (Jung, 1990: 54). It is as though the unconscious has breathed a huge sigh of relief that it no longer has to persistently knock on the door in the hope the dreamer will open it. Working on a recurring dream seems to keep the door open and make room for the layers underneath to manifest in further helpful dreams.

We have accepted that, however unwelcome, unresolved issues from the past that are affecting our current waking lives will regularly appear in our dreams and have taken to heart T. S. Eliot's lines from 'East Coker':

Not the intense moment isolated, with no before and after,
but a lifetime burning in every moment.
(Eliot, 1963: 203)

Trust and safety within the group is of paramount importance. So, after some initial experiences of sharing a personal dream and following much reflection, I decided it was not helpful to share my own dreams as I needed to facilitate and contain whatever was coming up both for the dreamer and the dreamworkers. Fortunately, I have other support outside the groups.

In effect the dreamworkers also hold the space for the dreamer, allowing the safe containment of unconscious contents. This offers us the freedom to work deeply with the dreams.

As the dreamwork developed we all realised that what might appear as entirely innocuous could often turn out to be a real challenge for the dreamer, opening up to public view shadow or unlived elements within the psyche the dreamer had no conscious idea of. The dreamer will then be encouraged to find an image to safely contain those elements and accompanying, potentially overwhelming, feelings.

> A visible enemy is always better than an invisible one.
> (Jung, 1989b: 57)

We learned that terrifying, threatening shadow figures rarely actually hurt the dreamer and through a guided return (see p. 32) into the dream could eventually be safely confronted or befriended and, if appropriate, integrated. The conscious integration of unconscious contents often releases power and energy within the dreamer's waking life as they embrace more of who they *really* are, including aspects they would rather not own. Over the years we have got to know each other extremely well!

A dreamer may have already thought of a title for the dream. If not, the group might ask the dreamer to come up with one quickly, without thinking about it, as the title often reveals the core message of the dream, but sometimes a specific title eludes the dreamer.

We acknowledge that, however irrelevant the content may appear, *every* part of the dream is important. There is always a reason, albeit sometimes inaccessible, *why* the unconscious has chosen, for instance, a red handbag, a dustbin or a particular time and setting.

Towards the end of working with someone's dream we usually leave time for a discussion of 'if this was my dream', which allows group members to summarise anything that might have stayed with them in response to the shared dream. Here we simply discuss whatever comes up, however irrelevant it may seem.

During this process and throughout every part of the dreamwork, the dreamer listens and watches out for any resonance (Sowton, 2013), particularly the somatic where something is powerfully felt in the body as a satisfying kind of 'coming together' within oneself. It is important for the *dreamer* to discern what fits and what doesn't, as other individual psyches can have their own influential reactions going on too. So it may be that only the dreamer feels the resonance, or both the dreamer *and* dreamworker(s) feel it, which often indicates an 'Aha!' moment of deep understanding. Sometimes only the *dreamworker* feels it, so here it is paramount that they are sufficiently self-aware to know that the resonance perhaps belongs only in *their* internal world. Conversely, something the dreamer rejects could be a defence against not wanting to admit it as a possibility.

While the defence is always respected, the dreamer is encouraged to 'let it cook' and see what emerges at some later date. If it *is* relevant the content will inevitably re-present itself for further consideration in another dream!

The archetypal images or collective motifs of a dream are often highlighted at this time, but we remind ourselves that an experience of an archetypal or collective image can be both objective and subjective and may well have relevance to the individual waking life of the dreamer.

Themes and contrasts will be shown in some of the individual dreams that follow.

Over time, we have learned to explore outside the confines of rationality by acknowledging our intuitive and somatic responses to the dream material and to pick up perceived puns, metaphors, and contrasts that may not have emerged during the initial dreamwork. This can be helpful to the dreamer, as puns and metaphors often open up further possibilities of understanding by showing that the symbol can contain a literal and hidden meaning at the same time.

For example, dreaming of underclothes covered by outer garments might also indicate *hidden aspects of Self* the dreamer would rather not show. A cobbled street could be a recognisable setting or something that is being *cobbled together*. My grandmother's will is perhaps my grandmother's *power* as well as her written will. A kitchen sink could show the dreamer has a *sinking feeling* about something or perhaps spends too much time at it. Washing up could mean there is something that is *washed up*, that needs to *be cleansed*, or is it simply a mundane task you are fed up with? Nakedness can be a fear of *being exposed* or maybe a desire to stop pretending. Being pregnant or giving birth can indicate a *previously unconscious part of Self coming into being*, or rarely that the dreamer either wishes to be or actually is unknowingly pregnant. Overflowing or unavailable toilets can show the urge to *get rid of unwanted psychic contents* or a more basic night-time urge to visit the loo.

The most frequent puns and metaphors seem to be images of and actions with heavy weights like suitcases, shopping baskets, holdalls and rucksacks, often alluding to the psychological *baggage* the dreamer is metaphorically carrying round with them.

If our offered insights into the puns and metaphors are to be effective *it is important that they have meaning for the dreamer.*

The group's collective energy sometimes seems to almost literally spark our imagination and intuition, which for me feels like fireworks exploding inside my head. These inner eruptions can be difficult to contain but, again, if the Roman Candle, Catherine Wheel or Crackerjack has no resonance for the dreamer we put it respectfully to one side.

We remember that:

> No dream symbol can be separated from the individual who dreams it, and there is no definite or straightforward interpretation of any dreams.
> (Jung, 1990: 53)

Our dreamwork is not exhaustive as a way of instantly accessing understanding and meaning, but more a slow process of discovery and integration that leaves the door open for further future insights. A dream can seem to be irrelevant at the time, but later, sometimes many years later, as life events unfold, such a dream can be understood with a clarity that almost mocks the original confusion. The dream finally reveals the answer to Jung's question, 'What is it *for*?'

We have also realised how helpful it can be to ask the 'right' question of the dreamer. This can sometimes be so obvious that no one has thought to offer it!

An example of this is described in Samantha's dream (see p. 43), where suddenly at the end of the dreamwork the right question was asked and the whole meaning of the dream was made much clearer. Another short dream shared by a group member describes an unwanted meeting with a controlling friend at a local pub. In response to statements made by the friend, the dreamer feels helpless and wants to scream. The 'right' question revealed the name of the pub as the Lion and the Lamb!

In the groups we often expand the dreamwork into an acting out of the dream either with the dreamer 'conducting' the re-enactment or, if preferred, being in the re-enactment so as to experience more fully, almost viscerally, the feeling and somatic response to the action. The 'actors' have the opportunity to dialogue with each other if this feels important.

Over the years, with the help of various props, our acting out has included shutting and opening doors, making frightening noises outside doors, murmuring in corners, crawling across the floor, lining up carrying broomsticks covered with sheets, dancing in the garden, wearing a top hat, looking at cobwebs above our heads, hiding behind sofas, befriending lions and tigers, falling down 'holes', dressing in black and white, offering 'forbidden fruit' in a bowl, marching up and down carrying a placard and tearing up and burning written words on the open fire.

We leave time for unpacking how it felt to every person taking part, as this can be really useful for the dreamer to understand how those different parts of themselves may be reacting unconsciously both to each other and to something in their waking life. We ensure that every participant is back in themselves and not left feeling as if they are someone else.[3]

It is not easy to convey in words the dynamism of working interactively in this way, so in the shared dreams that follow I have included only one acted out by a client in a one-to-one session (see Colin's dream, p. 52).

I have also found it almost impossible to express in words the depth at which we work in the groups, to describe the feelings and reactions that are so alive in the moment. Somehow to try and indicate every nuance, shift and realisation in words seems to detract from the experience.

---

3 If a dreamer enters a guided return into the dream or is taken through a visualisation or a re-enactment it is vital that they are firmly grounded afterwards. The dreamworker talks the dreamer through the exercise. The dreamer is asked to place both feet on the ground (floor) and breathe in deeply and slowly from the earth under their feet, through their body and out through the top of their head. Then, with the out breath, to come back down through the body and the feet, finally rooting themselves back in the earth. This is repeated three times and the dreamer is checked that they feel back in their body with a clear and secure sense of themselves. If this is not so the exercise is repeated.

Above all it is absolutely vital that dreamworkers in groups *and* psychotherapists in one-to-one work have a sufficiently strong Centre, and enough self-awareness, to know what belongs to them and what doesn't as, *especially in one-to-one work*, a dreamer can be very suggestible and harm can be done.

One-to-One Dreamwork in Psychotherapy

In one-to-one work with a client new to dreamwork and only the therapeutic hour in which to explore a dream, I work with the main images and feelings in the dream, ensuring that the work is left in a safe place. We can then, if appropriate, return to the dream in the following session. With clients who have been in therapy for a long time and who are fully engaged with the Individuation process, we work with the dream in the session and they continue the dreamwork at home. Putting aside the intellect, they use Jung's active imagination to dialogue with different parts, write, draw or play it out. This work can then be brought to the next session for further exploration.

> It does not suffice in all cases to elucidate only the conceptual context of a dream content. Often it is necessary to clarify a vague content by giving it a visible form. This can be done by drawing, painting or modelling. The hands will often solve a mystery the intellect has struggled with in vain.
> (Jung, 1966b: 181)

It feels important here to offer a word of warning about entering the dreamworld with our clients. We need to metaphorically and often literally have *our* feet firmly on the ground before we open the door to it. If either we or our clients cannot first find the door handle it is unwise to break down the door. There will always be a good reason why that 'little hidden door' remains shut.

> The dream is a little hidden door in the innermost and most secret recesses of the soul, opening into that cosmic night which was psyche long before there was ego consciousness, and which will remain psyche no matter how far our ego consciousness extends.
> (Jung, 1964a: 304)

The unconscious can be a dark and mysterious place to enter. Exploring unconscious material with a client who has serious mental health issues and insufficient ego strength to mediate what can be experienced as the intensity of the unconscious could lead to psychosis. It is therefore my view that working with their dreams is not appropriate.

If this is the case and a dream is brought to a session, I simply listen but do not explore it, apart from asking at the end how the client feels, then looking at and containing the feeling. Even having a dream just listened to, witnessed and received can bring a degree of relief to the dreamer without causing damage to their already fragile sense of Self.

> Lack of conscious understanding does not mean the dream has no effect at all ... Dreams can be understood to a certain extent in a subliminal way and *that is mostly how they work*.
> (Jung, 1977: 52, my emphasis)

4

The Invitation

Over the years many books have been written about dreams. Some are very academic, some offer definitive interpretations of particular symbols, while others focus only on one or two individual dreamers.

So why did I feel the need to write another? The answer, of course, is that it all started with a dream.

The Art and Architecture of the Renaissance

This is the dream that again stirred something that, prompted by The Golden Stone dream, had been brewing for many years in my unconscious. Again, I assiduously ignored what it was inviting me to bring into conscious action. It occurred around 6 a.m. in March 2016. The early morning appears to be my most active dreamtime.

Context

A friend had stayed the night on 4th March, ready to attend the dream group I was running the next day. We had chatted about the group and our dreamwork on Friday evening. I shared the dream over breakfast on 5th March. It was still vividly in my mind and paramount was the feeling of horror at the daunting prospect of talking about something I know nothing about. There was no time to work on the dream so it 'cooked' for a few days until there was space to look at it again.

Dream

I am in a classroom on the top floor of a school with Julia and Heidi. We are all present age and chatting about the talk Julia has just given. She picks up a printed programme and says, 'I didn't know you were giving a talk on the Art and Architecture of the Renaissance sometime in the not-too-distant future?'

I reply that I didn't know that either. I feel horrified, asking myself how I could have agreed, and say, 'But I don't know anything about it'.

I wake up somehow knowing that this dream is important.

Clarification and Amplification

I and others are present age. I am in the dream but cannot see what I am wearing.

The classroom: the classroom is a place of learning. I recognise it as the classroom I occupied in the last year of my grammar school education in 1959. It was on the top floor of a flagship school built shortly after the Second World War, the old school having been destroyed by bombing.

My education there was extremely academic with little room for creativity or individuality, unlike my primary school. The bombing of the old school and its replacement by a new building might symbolise the trajectory of my education.

Grammar school: could 'grammar' be a clue that the dream is about communicating something *written* correctly?

Question: my education is incomplete? What do I need to discover and learn in my present waking life that might further develop my self-awareness? Could the forthcoming talk to a wider public perhaps symbolise the waking up of something dormant in me? I have no idea to whom I am supposed to give the talk.

The top floor: the room is well lit with large windows letting in light. Might this indicate that something from the unconscious has ascended into relative consciousness, but I need to recognise that I cannot metaphorically 'leave school' until I have delivered the talk?

Julia and Heidi: two very close, supportive friends. One is a talented artist, the other a feng shui expert. Identical to their waking selves in the dream, they could be indicating they will offer support and encouragement in my endeavours. It is more likely they symbolise aspects of myself, the creative and the organiser of spaces.

Julia's response to my waking life request, 'What is art for you?' was:

> **A**ttention to observation
> **R**esonance in the heart
> **T**ransference into form.

This seems like the perfect discipline for creativity to emerge from the unconscious into consciousness and exactly what I need to write this book.

To quote Heidi: 'Feng shui is consciously creating a space that nurtures you, going with the flow and surrounded by things that nourish you.'

The inner and outer space needs to be thoroughly prepared so that the 'talk' can come to fruition.

The Julia part of me has already given her talk. This might show me a part of myself that at some level has already completed something?

The programme: have I been 'programmed' to present something? That I should do so is written down. The programme is printed in black and white (see 'Dream of the Cow/Bull', p. 15).

Julia's statement: 'I didn't know you were giving a talk on the Art and Architecture of the Renaissance?'

This reminds me of a spring meeting of the CJC some years ago. Browsing through the autumn programme, a friend sitting next to me remarked, 'I didn't know you were giving a talk in October?' I was really surprised and replied, 'Neither did I.' I had completely forgotten that several months earlier I had agreed to give a talk on alchemy, but there it was again in black and white.

The 'forgetting' is my tried and trusted way of putting something I do not want to do to one side and leaving it there gathering dust in my unconscious. I can still feel clearly the sinking feeling I experienced at the CJC that I had committed myself to this. Although alchemy is not an easy subject to talk about, I had then spent some 10 years studying it, whereas I know virtually nothing about the Art and Architecture of the Renaissance.

In contrast, the feeling in this dream is far more intense – I am absolutely *horrified*.

The talk: this feels symbolic of sharing something publicly. The idea of speaking in public fills me with deep apprehension, although the actual event is often surprisingly enjoyable, especially afterwards when it is all over! The feeling of *horror* in the dream shows me, despite years of working on it in therapy, just how deep the fear of 'getting it wrong' in front of others is.

But what is the talk? How could I have agreed to talk on a subject I know nothing about? At some level in the unconscious might I have agreed because I *did* know something about it? And is it possible that it could infer not an actual talk but some other form of communication, a book for example?

The Art and Architecture of the Renaissance: this title stayed with me for several days after the dream as I pondered upon it ('cooking' it in alchemical terms). Slowly it dawned on me that I had understood Renaissance as an historical time instead of its literal meaning – *rebirth*.

The *Oxford Dictionary* definition of art is 'a human skill as opposed to nature, skilful execution as an object in itself'; and of architecture, 'the art of the science of building'.

Now I began to see that for some 30 years, through training, personal therapy, supervision, dreamwork, alchemy and my work as a psychotherapist, I had actually been studying and experiencing both in my own life and those I work with that never-ending creative process of inner exploration to discover who we truly are – our rebirth.

Alchemy, often referred to as the art of the Egyptians, is a source of ancient wisdom long lost to our consciousness and subsumed by the church as heresy. To quote Jung:

> Alchemy is rather like an undercurrent to the Christianity that ruled on the surface. It is to this surface as the dream is to consciousness, and just as the dream compensates the conflicts of the conscious mind, so alchemy endeavours to fill the gaps left open by the Christian tension of opposites.
> (Jung, 1989a: 23)

Outwardly, alchemy is seen as an attempt to turn base metal into gold, but its true meaning for the alchemists, and later for Jung, is the transformative inner work from relative unconsciousness to a greater consciousness of our ultimate destination of finding within ourselves the real gold of the true self – his concept of Individuation.

Unlike the alchemists we are perhaps so mesmerised by our own experience that we do not often explore what that experience is *for* and remain in ignorance. But, if we follow their example and engage with the inner processes, it offers the opportunity to creatively grow out of who we believe we are and begin to build up into who we really are.

Once I had understood the Art and Architecture of the Renaissance in a less literal way – dreams are rarely literal – I slowly realised that perhaps, after all, I might know something about it. I began to understand that working with dreams could be experienced as an art and they are, perhaps, one of the architects of our *rebirth* into wholeness.

The dream clearly shows my resistance to that knowing and my reluctance to try and describe it in words; once verbal or written it would be there for myself and others to judge, and be found wanting.

Aftermath

Two weeks after the dream I attended a previously arranged session with Paul Lambillion, an internationally known spiritual teacher and author. Without my mentioning the dream, or anything at all about writing, Paul suggested that part of my work here might be an invitation to write a book. There was an 'Aha!' moment as I understood this could be the 'talk' I was programmed to give.

Update: December 2020

Nearly five years on and, although much of the work is done, the resistance has been formidable – I would qualify for a master's degree in displacement activity – but it underlines how, in the dreamworld, time and space take place in a different dimension, patiently awaiting our conscious engagement when resistance has been recognised and overcome.

Having finally accepted the 'invitation' to get my scribblings on to the computer, I spent the last two days of 2020 on my laptop. It felt like something had switched on in my brain and at last I felt engaged with the process. Closing the document I was working on, I checked emails before a quick lunch break. On my return I simply could not open any of the documents in my files, although everything else was accessible. Eventually I gave up, switched off the laptop and went for a walk.

So, what was going on? Years ago, during a very cold January, while reluctantly preparing a talk on alchemy for the CJC, the room radiator would not turn off despite the thermostat being turned to 0. I had been writing about 'cooking' the inner contents and sure enough I cooked, almost literally. When the writing was finished, the radiator turned itself off and has never been a problem since.

Now, in writing about my resistance I could not access the file to continue. Was my resistance so unconsciously powerful that I had somehow 'shut down' that access? Once those ideas were more conscious, I returned to the computer, opened it up and had no difficulty in accessing the file!

I am reminded again of Jung's concept of synchronicity, where there is no barrier between the inner and the outer, psyche and matter, the one reflecting the other, often in a physical manifestation.

Since then, there seems to have been a big shift and, instead of resisting the process, I appear to have embraced it, as the 'log jam' dispersed, the writing flowed and the book has taken shape.

If this book interests you and you would like to explore further, there are some suggestions at the end for keeping a dream journal (see p. 132), some ideas for working with dreams many of which have been used in the dreams that follow (see p. 43), and a recommended reading list (see p. 148). I would particularly like to recommend Robert Johnson's excellent book "Inner Journey" as a follow on to "Wake up to your Dreams".

Although every dreamer has given their permission for their dreams to be shared, to maintain confidentiality all names and some details have been changed.

The dreamwork is a *co-operation* between the dreamer and the dreamworker(s), with the dreamer always encouraged to interact with their own response to each part of the dreamwork. For the sake of brevity, this reaction has been mainly summarised at the end of the dreamwork.

Should you find that any of the dreams described stir up difficult memories or experiences for you, please seek the help of an experienced psychotherapist familiar with dreamwork who can help you to understand more fully that which lies unresolved in your unconscious.

I hope these dreams will offer you a glimpse of the richness and inspiration to be found in our nightly excursions into the dreamworld and encourage you to undertake your own explorations into that world, accompanied by a trusted guide.

5

The Explorations

Samantha's Dream

> The prospective function ... is an anticipation in the unconscious of future conscious achievement, something like a preliminary exercise or sketch, or a plan roughed out in advance.
>
> *(Jung, 1970b: 493)*

This is a dream from a member of a dream group. It was used in a workshop for trainee counsellors where, having shared the context and the dream, my co-presenter (D) and I (G) acted out a very condensed version of the original group dreamwork.

Context

The dream occurred some time ago. The dreamer is an experienced therapist in her forties who was struggling with the idea of engaging with further professional qualifications, as she felt she had a lack of early education and had little confidence in her ability to undertake the process. She could feel something almost *pulling* her towards the next step, but she resisted it.

Dream

The dreamer has been given a ticket for a concert in a local theatre. She is on her way but has been delayed and is running late. When she arrives at the theatre the concert has already started and the theatre is packed with unknown people. She knows that she needs to be at the front and shoulders her way forwards so that she is just in front of the stage. A band member sees her, comes towards her, reaches out his hand and pulls her up on to the stage. Suddenly the dreamer is in the spotlight with the band. She feels really surprised, but oddly comfortable.

Dreamwork

The group asked the dreamer how she felt having just shared the dream. Samantha thought for a moment and then said, 'I feel bemused.'

We then went through the processes of clarification and amplification in the sequence of the dream, summarised as follows:

G. (as dreamworker(s)) Are you in the dream or observing or both?
D. (as dreamer) Very much *in* the dream particularly pushing my way forward, which feels unlike me but OK.
G. How old are you in the dream?
D. Present age.
G. Can you see what you are wearing?
D. Not really, but probably the sort of thing I would wear to a concert, casual and comfortable.
G. Are you feeling comfortable in the dream?
D. No, more bothered.
G. What was the delay?
D. It could have been something to do with the family.
G. In waking life is that something that happens sometimes?

- D. Stuff often gets put on hold.
- G. How does it feel to be 'running late'?
- D. Not good, a bit anxious and frustrated.
- G. Do you recognise the theatre?
- D. No, but in the dream I think it's local.
- G. How does it feel that the concert has already started?
- D. I feel cross that I've missed some of it.
- G. In waking life is there any sense that you are late for something that has already started?
- D. Yes, it's a familiar feeling.
- G. Do you recognise any of the other people?
- D. No, but they are a mixture of ages and gender.
- G. What is the feeling when you get to the front?
- D. Satisfaction.
- G. How does it feel when a band member pulls you up on to the stage?
- D. Amazing.
- G. In the dream you feel surprised to be there but oddly comfortable in the spotlight. If this was to happen in waking life, would you feel the same?
- D. Absolutely not, I would be very embarrassed and want to run off the stage.
- G. What is the strongest feeling in the dream?
- D. Pushing my way forwards.
- G. How does that feel?
- D. I'm very determined. It feels good.
- G. Would you push yourself forward like that in waking life?
- D. No, I'd hang around at the back wishing I could be at the front.
- G. Do you have any sense of what the dream is trying to show you?
- D. Not really, I still feel bemused but I know it is important.

If This Was My Dream ...

We then went round the group with 'if this was my dream' and members came up with several ideas, for example,

'I'd be thinking about the ticket I have that allows me entrance to something I really want to go to.'

'I'd be feeling angry that my family – possibly an internalised family – seems to be holding me back from something that I really want to do.'

'I'd be struck by knowing that I'm late for something.'

'I'd be thinking about my clothes and how I've chosen to be comfortable and casual.'

'I'd be wondering about all those unknown people and how they might be different aspects and ages of me that have already found their way to the venue but could be holding me back from getting to where I need to be.'

'I'd be wanting to get to know better the part of me that *can* push her way forward and is willing to let a masculine (animus) part of me put me "centre stage" and is OK with being in the spotlight. I'd also be asking, has the stage been set for something?'

'I'd notice how some of my responses seem to reflect my conscious feeling about further qualifications.'

At this point in the group interaction I could feel my intuition prompting me to ask another question, which had not come up during the dreamwork. So I said, 'If this was my dream, I'd be asking, what is the name of the band?'

With a sudden jolt of understanding and resonance for the dreamer the answer came – 'U2,' she said.

The dream group just fell about laughing as we all resonated with what the dream was trying to convey to Samantha – that she too, despite all delays from internal and external pressures, could safely push her way forward to the next stage, not just in her career but in her inner process towards Individuation, becoming more of who she really is.

Outcome

Within a year of having this prognostic dream and almost out of the blue, the dreamer was invited (as she was invited on to the stage) to study for a prestigious qualification. She has since achieved this qualification, surprising herself by how well she has done and gaining in confidence. The dreamer embodied and lived the dream symbols.

We can see from this dream how Samantha's unconscious was compensating for her conscious attitude to further education in trying to show her the possibilities that were in front of her and that she could, despite the delay and her misgivings and lack of confidence, embrace this next part of her life wholeheartedly, if she actively engaged with the process.

Active engagement can lead to the dream being fulfilled in the dreamer's waking life, although the timing may not be what we think it should be. The unconscious then breathes a metaphorical sigh of relief, as working with a dream and bringing it to fruition clears the way for further revelations and inner processes to develop.

Update

On rereading the dream recently, Samantha was amazed at its accurate portrayal of where she was in her life then and how the dream had been fulfilled so quickly and unexpectedly.

Heather's Dream: The Seven Pillars of Wisdom

A dream of a very experienced psychotherapist approaching her seventies, explored some years ago in a dream group.

Context

This dream arrived a short while before Heather had to make an important decision either to continue teaching or retire from it and concentrate on private practice. In addition, many demanding family commitments surrounded the dreamer in her waking life.

Dream

It is a bright, sunny, calm day. I am standing looking at a ruin of a classical temple with paving stones on the ground and fluted pillars either side, with a sense of the pillars going on quite a way ahead of me.

There is no roof and the feeling is one of great space. I say out loud, 'Oh this is what I want. I want to move into this space.'

The dreamer wakes up feeling calm and relaxed, but with a sense of longing.

Group Dreamwork

The title was arrived at towards the end of the dreamwork. According to the Institute for Creation Research, a 'life of genuine wisdom' is supported by 'purity, peaceableness, gentleness, reasonableness, helpfulness, humility and sincerity' – the Seven Pillars of Wisdom (Morris, 2008).

The dreamer is present age and in the dream throughout and, although not observing from outside the dream, she is passive not active.

The main feeling was of calm and expansiveness.

One-word feeling reaction from group members: (this is sometimes invited immediately after the dreamer has finished sharing the dream, giving the dreamer affirmation, insight and perhaps challenges to ponder on): 'peace', 'calm', 'longing', 'coming home', 'relaxed', 'ruined'.

Heather could relate to all of these reactions.

Clarification and Amplification

Heather felt the **setting** was ancient or timeless, possibly in Greece. It was outside, rural and brightly lit by the sun. The dreamer felt it was summertime and perhaps afternoon.

There is no one else in the dream.

The paving stones: a soft grey, providing solid ground for Heather to stand on.

The pillars: a warm sandstone, strong enough to withstand the passage of time but without a roof to provide protection. The temple, as Heather felt it was, has fallen into some disrepair.

Rural and brightly lit: likely to show an organic process is taking place with the sun of consciousness illuminating the process.

At this point in the dreamwork we asked Heather if she could re-enter the dream and to relive the experiences in it:

> *I feel supported by the paving stones, the air is warm and kind around me. I feel welcome here. The pillars seem to stretch into infinity but with a sense of perspective. The space is clean and clear without boundaries of time but the pillars also contain the space, so it feels safe.*
>
> *I feel sad that the temple is a ruin, but there is enough of it left for it still to be a beautiful place and without the roof it feels open to the world around me.*

> *I am not sure whether this is the end or beginning of something.*
>
> *This is a place of respite and renewal and it is exactly what I need.*

Heather then felt more aware of her sadness, but also of the ancient peace within this space.

Having ensured Heather was back in the present moment (see p. 32), we went round the group with 'if this was my dream'.

If This Was My Dream ...

'I'd be feeling sure of my ground and that the paving stones could be paving the way for something yet to happen' (possible use of pun by the unconscious).

'I'd wonder if this was a place within myself that I've neglected for too long so that it appears to be outside and foreign to myself but is still within reach?'

'I'd be feeling a bit isolated here.'

'I'd realise that here I could gain a sense of perspective in my life.'

'I would like to walk into the distance leaving everything behind me and never come back.'

'I'd be wondering what I might have neglected that lies in ruins and is it possible to rebuild it?'

'I'd be reassured there is still enough of the temple left for me to go there.'

'I'd ask myself if the temple could be a symbol of the Self?'

'I'd suggest that this dream of a calm, peaceful place could be compensating for the demands and intensity of my waking life.'

'I might recognise that I demonstrate all the qualities of the Seven Pillars of Wisdom towards others but perhaps I don't offer them to myself?'

(The group's experience of Heather is that she does indeed uphold the Seven Pillars of Wisdom.)

Heather resonated with all these statements apart from feeling isolated, as she realised that what she wanted and needed most was enough space for herself without commitments to others intruding on her busy life.

The group looked at how the dreamer could revisit this beautiful but neglected temple within herself to replenish her energy and regain a sense of balance in her life, so that necessary external commitments could be managed in a way less damaging to her well-being.

Outcome

Heather resigned from the teaching commitment and felt immediate relief, showing she had listened to the dream. The commitments to others are ongoing and the dreamer can struggle to reconnect with her inner temple of peace, but holds on to the knowledge that it is always there within herself.

Update

Heather subsequently experienced the protracted illness and loss of two close family members and had to let go of many other commitments. She now finds that with more space opening up in her life she actively seeks that temple of peace within herself that, in time, may offer the possibility of healing and renewal.

Colin's Recurring Dreams

To experience a dream ... is very different from having a tepid rehash set before you on paper (Jung 1966a: 199)

Colin was in his late thirties and had been in weekly therapy with me for about 18 months. There were issues within his dysfunctional family where Colin had suffered a degree of childhood neglect. He had introjected strong parental messages about expressing feelings that were neither understood nor allowed. Colin realised at a young age that he was gay, but he had difficulty in forming relationships.

We had just begun to work with his dreams when he shared a recurring nightmare that had started when he was around 8 years old. The age of 8 is typical of early childhood memories as it is a time when the child can begin to recognise and work out that all might not be well within the family. The nightmare recurred regularly throughout his life, especially when he was exhausted and, at a time of recent family crisis, it had returned to haunt him once again.

Dream 1

I am asleep in my bedroom where I live now. I wake up to find a horrible goblin/troll in my room. He is dancing wildly round the room with a chopper in his hand.

The dreamer wakes from the dream feeling anxious and frightened.

Dreamwork

Colin is present age and in a current setting. The atmosphere is dark with a sense of imminent threat. The main feeling in the dream is terror of what the goblin/troll might do if he started to attack.

In the dream Colin is *asleep* – in other words metaphorically unconscious. He *wakes up* – not actually but in the dream – indicating that the dream content is coming more into consciousness. There is something Colin's dream maker wants him to be really aware of. The dream maker seems to be that mysterious part of our psyche that creates our nightly adventures in the world of dreams.

The goblin/troll: is small, terrifying and out of control. He reminded Colin of the gnomes in the garden centres where he was often left on his own as a young child while his mother went shopping elsewhere. This was a frightening experience as Colin never knew when his mother would return to collect him.

Dancing wildly: is not something Colin would ever do as it would feel out of control not knowing where it might lead.

The chopper: Colin related this to chopping wood – a familiar activity in his childhood – but also to the chopper being potentially an offensive weapon.

At this point in the dreamwork I could feel a growing sense that it might be helpful to act out the dream within the safety of the therapeutic container. Somehow, I knew it would be safe to do so. I excused myself from the room and returned with a real and substantial chopper.

I asked the dreamer to connect with the goblin/troll and see what it felt like to become him. I handed Colin the chopper. Colin began to look different, with an expression of wily cunning and glee on his face as he began to dance wildly round the room, waving the chopper around. He made energetic slashing movements, letting out shouts of triumph.

For the first time in his life Colin felt he had been given permission to express his true feelings.

The energy slowly dissipated. Colin sat down and handed back the chopper. We looked at each other and began to laugh. 'How did that feel?' I asked. 'Wonderful, exhilarating, freeing,' he replied.

To ensure Colin was back in himself we did a grounding exercise (see p. 32). This is really important as experiences like this can be very powerful and the client needs to be able to function on returning to the outside world after the session.

Thoughts Shortly After the Dreamwork

Dreamwork is not usually exhaustive as a way of instantly accessing meaning, but more of a slow process of discovery and integration.

I felt that the goblin/troll could be a primitive, mythological part of Colin that had been shut down by his parents in childhood and had retreated into the unconscious. This part wanted to break out and express its rage, using the chopper to cause serious damage to his surroundings and perhaps to others and even himself. The nightmare emerged around the age of 8 when the dreamer would have been more aware of his feelings but had nowhere to safely express them.

As Jung stated, the dream is often compensatory to our conscious waking attitude to who we think we are. Here the nightmare reveals the rage beneath Colin's gentle caring nature.

I shared these thoughts with Colin, who found a resonance to them within himself.

After working with this dream Colin slowly began to express more of his long bottled-up anger, frustration and power, both within the therapy and in his waking life. To do so before would have carried the threat of isolation, abandonment and the feeling that he was unlovable. As the feelings became known to Colin and owned by him it gradually no longer felt so dangerous to express them.

This dream has never returned to haunt Colin.

Shortly after the dreamwork above, as Colin settled down to sleep, he invited his dream maker to open up further insight into his inner world.

He then experienced another familiar recurring dream which had started some five years ago at a time of relational turmoil in his life.

Dream 2

I am on a familiar well-worn track across a field. A 10-foot-high brick wall runs all the way alongside the track. Some undergrowth is spilling on to the path in places. I am aware I am part of a group. It feels reassuring, but I cannot actually see anyone. I am looking for creatures, although previously I have never found any.

For the first time on this path I come across some steel traps and need to disable them with sticks. There are about six of them and they are obvious, not hidden.

Then a Neanderthal man appears on the track, dark and very hairy with a ginger beard. I am now above the scene and the wall has disappeared. I now want to meet the man.

Dreamwork

Colin is present age and the main feeling in the dream is curiosity.

The track: is similar to one he walks on not far from where he lives and works. The track is well worn, so it is a place that the dreamer actually and metaphorically journeys along regularly.

A field: the way forward traverses a field, perhaps alluding to a 'field of dreams'?

The brick wall: Colin felt this was 'walling him in' so that he could not see what was on the other side. The wall is 10-feet high, so there is a possibility that for survival the dreamer erected a 'wall' between himself and the outside world when he was about 10 years old. A brick wall can protect but also be a metaphor, as in 'I'm up against a brick wall' or 'I've hit a brick wall'.

The undergrowth: this is an interesting word as it literally means something growing under something else, often hiding what is underneath. The undergrowth has *over*grown on to the path in places. We thought undergrowth could symbolise unconscious contents that had begun to spill into consciousness but threatened to obscure the way forward unless cleared.

The group: although Colin cannot see anyone, he is aware of being part of something that feels reassuring. The group itself might represent different aspects of the dreamer that are coming into awareness, potentially perhaps to create a new internal family.

Creatures: Colin is looking for something he has never found, possibly the instinctual parts of himself that were shut off in childhood.

The steel traps: these were not seen previously in this recurring dream, so has something new emerged from the unconscious or were the traps there before, hidden by the undergrowth but have now (through the dreamwork) become clearly visible?

Colin needs to disable the traps and uses sticks to do so. It feels essential to do this. There are six of them, perhaps indicating that at 6 years old Colin became more conscious of the psychological and emotional 'traps' set – probably by his parents – for those instinctual unwary parts, or they could have been set by Colin to try and kill off the 'unacceptable' parts of himself before they could cause a problem.

If the dreamer does not disable the traps they will still lie in wait for him in the future.

The Neanderthal man: it is only *after the traps have been disabled* that the man appears. He is hairy and wild. We explored the possibility that he was a shadow figure, a more primitive unlived part of Colin, grounded in nature and who knows how to survive in a hostile world. Colin warmed to this idea.

Above the scene: Colin has moved from the subjective position to the objective, he is above the scene and can see more of the whole picture. More of his internal dreamworld has emerged into consciousness.

We felt the disappearance of the wall was self-explanatory.

Colin wants to meet the man. I asked the dreamer to visualise this and he wanted to take his hand and let him take him to meet his family.

It seems that when we ignore the *appearance* of ugliness and befriend the seemingly 'grotesque' in our dreams we can receive the life-giving gift of the transformation of part of ourselves.

The desire to meet the man's family showed us the dreamer's archetypal need for belonging, to feel he was loved and acceptable. Perhaps the dream explores the possibility that Colin needed to start within himself, finding a way to belong in his own internal family?

Outcome

Colin diligently worked through the increasingly difficult dynamics in his birth family and came to a much more settled place about the past and the present. He began to access and express his feelings more freely and become much more comfortable with who he really is.

Colin is now in a loving and stable relationship.

Update

In response to my request for Colin's permission to use these dreams, and even though the dreams occurred several years ago, the rereading of them prompted Colin to do further work on them. As

Colin is now a very experienced dreamer, this work was completed on his own and is in his own words, as follows:

Colin's Dreamwork

I'm actually quite struck reading them again with the progression of one dream into the other and each containing so many 'primitive' references.

The goblin: I think he could also be a mischievous part of me that was never allowed to be expressed as I wanted. I was constrained by my parents' ideas of how I should behave, and dancing freely with gay abandon was not one of them.

The chopper or axe: is an ancient tool, probably one of the first made by early hunter-gatherers. It has the potential to nourish and nurture by providing food and wood for warmth but can also be used in battle. I see it as quite a powerful masculine symbol and I am fearful of embracing it as the goblin does in the dream. In the dream I can only see the potential for harm as I am laid out helplessly on the bed and fear being mutilated, dismembered or sacrificed.

I now wonder if that fear is also related to the process of Individuation and the taking apart and reintegration that had started in the therapy?

I also get 'axe to grind', which for me is that feeling of knowing something to be true, but without evidence, and wanting everyone to know that truth. 'Bury the hatchet' could be to make peace with something or someone [perhaps Colin himself?].

In order to act, I needed permission to take control of the chopper that was given to me in the dreamwork.

The Neanderthal man: was a primitive hunter-gatherer, now extinct, but a predecessor whose DNA is still present in modern man. Walking 'the ancestral path' in the dream I encounter the

Neanderthal and feel a need to connect with him. In my waking life, I had an often absent father so never felt protected or nurtured. I was left without effective leadership and controlled through fear. The Neanderthal part of me could provide that protection.

The steel traps: these were new to this recurring dream and only appeared after the dreamwork with the goblin. Again, like the chopper, they held the potential to inflict instantaneous damage but also the slow protracted agony of being trapped while being vulnerable to others.

I also now wonder if, following the dreamwork, further unconscious fears that I had previously had to 'keep the trap shut on' had emerged from the undergrowth. Prior to being in therapy, 'keeping my trap shut' would have been my default mechanism in dealing with problems but, in the course of our work together, it felt safe and actually essential to engage with and disable those traps just as it did with the chopper.

(There is another important personal and collective dream of Colin's later in the book, see p. 111.)

The Snippet

A snippet of an image or perhaps two words or just a feeling will sometimes be remembered by the dreamer on waking. We have learned the value of respecting and working with snippets as they often reveal much more than we expected. Group work can be particularly effective as we all give our response to what has been shared, helping the dreamer to enlarge upon the snippet and its meaning for them.

Amelia's Snippet

Amelia is a psychotherapist in her forties, a long-standing member of a dream group and an established single mother with family commitments.

The dreamer had woken up with two words: **roller coaster.** There was no image, person or any other information.

Amelia felt bemused on waking. The group then responded with their own brief feeling reaction to the two words: 'funfair', 'terror', 'excitement', 'feeling sick', 'panic', 'out of control'.

The dreamer resonated most with 'panic' and 'out of control'.

We asked Amelia to visualise a roller coaster and what it felt like to be on one. Initially she thought it was supposed to be a fun experience, but then felt herself whizzing through different 'rooms' so quickly she couldn't take anything in. Then she began to feel sick, panic and realise that she couldn't get off the roller coaster until the 'person in charge' stopped it. We then encouraged Amelia to find that inner figure, take control, get off the 'ride' and feel the ground under her feet. Amelia immediately stopped spinning and felt safely back in the room again.

This visualisation led to wondering if there was anything in Amelia's waking life that matched the frantic up-and-down, out-of-control experience?

After a moment the dreamer realised that this was exactly how her current waking life felt, as if in all areas of her life (perhaps the 'rooms'?) she was going up and down on a roller coaster that she believed she had no power to stop.

The group asked Amelia if she would like to share what she felt the roller coaster of her life consisted of. She reflected on this and came up with many of the life events around her that seemed to have taken over.

We asked the question, 'What would it feel like in waking life to stop the roller coaster and get off it?' Amelia felt there would be huge relief in doing this. The group then added how they might react:

'I'd feel I was taking back control.'

'It would be good to find my feet on the ground again.'

'I'd stop being taken for a ride.'

'I'd wonder about the part of me that takes over and won't let me stop.'

'I'd be thinking about what presents itself to me as something potentially enjoyable, but I realise it isn't.'

'I'd look forward to leaving the roller coaster behind.'

The input from the group helped Amelia to see that if she could do further inner work on the operator of the roller coaster within her she could then make different, more helpful choices about the direction of her life.

Outcome

Amelia carefully made the necessary changes in her waking life and eventually got off the roller coaster and found a calmer and more fulfilling way of life.

Update

In response to my recent request for Amelia's permission to use this dream she emailed me:

'Rereading the dream I've seen how far I have come since that moment. I have learned to take control of my life/things and value myself enough to say no and take care of my needs. To do what I need to do, to not be taken on an out-of-control ride.'

Beatrice's Dream

Beatrice is a psychotherapist in her fifties and a dream group member. After the break-up of a difficult and coercive relationship of many years, she is beginning to find a new and fulfilling direction in her life.

Context

The evening before this dream Beatrice had accompanied me to the CJC to watch a video replay of a talk on alchemy I had given some years earlier. Alchemy was unknown territory for the dreamer.

Dream

I'm present age and in the dream not observing it. A male voice, not very clear, says, 'Alice, let's cook'. I am walking along a path by a river on my right. The water is fast flowing in the opposite direction to the way I'm walking. It is daylight.

On waking from the dream, Beatrice recalled that the day before she had gone for a walk in an unfamiliar place and got lost. There were several rabbit holes on the path and she had almost fallen down one. She realised she needed to return to the solid ground she had started out from and found her way back. There was no sense of being lost in the dream.

Group Dreamwork

We did not go round the group to share our feeling reaction to this dream.

Clarification and Amplification

The male voice: is not recognisable to Beatrice but, as previously described (see p. 5), a voice on its own usually brings an important message to the dreamer. The voice here is not very distinct but still audible. This might show that the message from the unconscious is not being clearly heard.

'Alice, let's cook': Beatrice's association to this was the middle name of a relative and Alice who disappears down a rabbit hole in *Alice in Wonderland*, but this was not a book she liked.

At this point the dreamer and I remembered an illustration (see overleaf) – 'The Mountain of the Adepts' – that I had used in the talk the previous evening. Part of the illustration shows what looks like a rabbit at the foot of the mountain about to disappear down a rabbit hole. This is to show the seeker that the right way to engage with the alchemical journey towards the realisation of the Self – Individuation – is to follow your instinct – the rabbit – into the dark, unknown interior of the mountain, the inner world of the unconscious leading to the philosopher's stone.

I had also mentioned how this process has to be 'cooked' within oneself. The ingredients for the work need to be 'heated up' through much inner engagement, usually over a very long period of time, before greater self-awareness emerges slowly from the 'oven' of the unconscious.

The words in the dream sounded like an invitation, but to Beatrice they came across as an instruction.

The river on my right: is unfamiliar with clear, fast-flowing water bubbling over rocks. The river is boundaried and contained, almost like a canal. On the right could indicate arriving in consciousness and/or right brain as the emotional, feeling and intuitive aspect dominating the left brain as the more logical, analytical, thinking aspect.

Water often symbolises the unconscious. Here the water is clear, so the possibly dangerous rocks in the inner world can be easily seen. The water is rushing over them, carrying itself to its destination – the ocean – perhaps symbolising the collective unconscious.

The waters from the unconscious are not out of control but flow within an obvious and dedicated container, perhaps the dreamer's increasingly strong Centre.

The opposite direction: Beatrice questioned why she was not 'going with the flow' and 'going against the current' (possibly a pun

Mountain of the Adepts containing the Philosopher's Stone. Engraving from Stephen Michelspacher's 'Alchemia' 1654

meaning present events?). Could it be that unconsciously she was starting to go against *other people's perceptions* of who she really is? Did this reflect something she was already doing in waking life? This did not feel wrong in the dream and the dreamer realised that, as in the alchemical process talked about the previous evening, perhaps she needed to hold within herself these opposites of trying to be what others appeared to want while holding on to being her emergent true self. This accurately reflected Beatrice's current internal world where she was struggling with opposing feelings about the ending of the relationship. The dreamer felt she needed to learn to trust the process.

Just at this moment of acknowledgement in the dreamwork the sun, hidden behind clouds all morning, shone into the room directly on to Beatrice, as if to say, 'Yes, this is the light of understanding that you need.' The group experienced this as a reassuring synchronistic event.

Observations: on her walk in waking life, Beatrice had realised that if she fell down a rabbit hole she was entirely alone without help. She felt this was echoed in perhaps fearing this journey on her own into the unconscious, where she might not see the danger and get injured.

If This Was My Dream ...

'I'd be thinking about looking through the keyhole, which means that at the moment I can't see all of what is happening to me.'

'I'd be wondering why I'm walking against the current and questioning whether I'm on the right path.'

'I'd be reassured that I can see clearly what is under the water.'

'I'd be feeling that whatever I'm doing it's OK.'

'I'd be reassured that I'm not on my own as the group will be there for me if I fall down a rabbit hole.'

'I'd want to reread *Alice in Wonderland* with the emphasis on *Wonder*land.'

Beatrice resonated with much of the above, seeing the possibilities for moving forward that her dream was trying to show her.

Outcome

The dreamer could not find her original copy of *Alice in Wonderland* so somewhat reluctantly bought another one. This copy somehow got 'lost' and was not found until a long time after the dream, but Beatrice is still resisting reading it!

Could there be unlived shadow aspects of herself hidden deep in the story and character of Alice in *Alice in Wonderland*?

What is Beatrice's wonderland and how can she differentiate between what is fantasy and what is real? The inner journey is a lifetime's work.

However, with courage and perseverance she continues to try and hold the opposites within herself and 'cook' the dream content, bringing about huge beneficial changes in her life and emerging as the person she truly is.

Update

The night after rereading her dream Beatrice had another dream and recalled one very vivid part of it:

> *I am diving down into clear water, swimming and looking for a way out and finding the opening and swimming into fresh air. There is no sense of alarm at all.*

Beatrice is present age in the dream and feels it might be showing her that, since the original dream, there had been a clearing of some unconscious contents and a definite movement upward towards a way out from where she had been at the time of the 'Alice' dream. She now feels she is going with the flow of her real self (even if that is against the current of outside opinion), and, as in this dream, *is* emerging into that 'fresh' air.

Become what you have always been, namely, the wholeness we have lost in the midst of our civilised, conscience existence,

> a wholeness that we always were without knowing it.
> (Jung, 1970a: 722)

Timothy's Dream

> The darkness which clings to every personality is the door into the unconscious and the gateway of dreams, from which these two twilight figures, the shadow and the anima step into our nightly visions.
> (Jung, 1981: 123)

Timothy is a client in his late sixties who had a series of dreams over a long period about a female figure, sometimes known and sometimes unknown. These figures were often shadowy, indicating that they were probably symbolising an unconscious feminine aspect of the dreamer that Jung called the 'anima'. This is one of Timothy's later dreams:

> *I'm on my way to meet a woman/therapist with whom I have an appointment. I feel in a bit of a hurry. I enter into an unknown building that is somewhat old and gloomy. Upstairs I go in to a rather dark, dusty room, which is empty apart from a woman who looks like someone I know. She is sitting in a wooden chair and is wearing a navy-blue cardigan buttoned up to the neck. She wants to talk to me, but I say I can't stay as I have to go away on my honeymoon.*

Timothy woke feeling curious and relieved.

Initial Collaborative Exploration and Ideas

The dreamer felt that in the dream he was in his thirties/forties, an age range that occurred frequently in his dreams. It had been a time of significant life transition.

Timothy has a prearranged meeting, indicating an obligation, to meet with a woman on the first floor of an unknown, neglected building. This might show that something is finding its way up from the unconscious, often symbolised by the ground floor or basement, into some degree of consciousness – the first floor.

The woman, almost certainly an anima figure (a feminine part of the dreamer), is waiting for him in the empty room. The dusty unvisited room shows she has been waiting a long time for Timothy and she is not comfortable on the basic wooden chair. She is also 'buttoned up' in the navy cardigan. This could be a pun for the anima figure's reaction to the dreamer's neglect of her. She has become cold and withdrawn but would still like to talk to the dreamer.

The anima, possibly also representing Timothy's inner therapist, wants to open up a dialogue with him but he pulls away, eager to set off on his honeymoon.

The dreamer felt he wanted to leave as quickly as possible and not engage in conversation with the woman. There was a strong sense of urgency about needing to go on his honeymoon.

At this point I observed that for a honeymoon to happen it is usual for a marriage to have first taken place!

For Timothy, a honeymoon is the nice part after all the hassle of getting married is over and he can go away on holiday with his beloved, leaving everyone else behind.

This idea is strongly reflected in the dream, as it looks as though the dreamer is trying to avoid the daunting prospect of uniting with his inner feminine side by rushing off to the next stage before the first is completed. The avoidance is perhaps reflected in his waking feeling of *relief.*

Timothy needed to engage in that conversation with the feminine within, so I suggested that perhaps he tried to return to the room. Here he could listen to what she wanted to say and how he wished to respond, while noting his reactions to the conversation. This was work to be done at home.

The dreamer was currently experiencing a sense of urgency in his waking life that echoed the changes and choices he made in his thirties and forties, when it felt there was more work he needed to do. Although this was relevant, it felt the dream was also trying to show Timothy that the *inner* work of uniting with his feminine side was equally urgent and important. No honeymoon period could take place without the union of opposites, where masculine and feminine come together within the dreamer's psyche in the alchemical *Coniunctio*.

In dreamwork, thoughts and images come to mind perhaps long after the dream has been shared, hence the following:

Later Clarification and Amplification

The setting: Timothy did not recognise the urban street he was in nor the building or room he entered. He is in an unfamiliar neglected psychic space.

Time of day: it could have been late in the day as everything is dark and gloomy. This might show the dreamer that time is getting on for him to do the necessary inner work, but what needs to be done has been tucked away in a dark unlit corner of his psyche.

The appointment: Timothy's dream maker has prepared the psychic space for the dreamer to attend this important meeting.

The woman: reminded Timothy of a psychotherapist he had once been close to but had not seen for a long time.

The wooden chair: the anima figure is waiting for the dreamer to keep his appointment with her on something that is timeless but offers little ease.

The cardigan: was not something that person would have worn but as a possible anima figure she could feel 'buttoned up' by Timothy.

Interestingly, on the day of the dreamwork *I* was wearing a navy cardigan, without buttons, and I am a psychotherapist. Could it be that Timothy experienced *me* as being potentially 'buttoned up' in the work we were doing or that he would prefer it if I was?

The conversation: the dreamer wants to avoid any contact with the woman that might lead to a greater, and perhaps challenging, engagement with her.

The honeymoon: Timothy unconsciously wants to avoid the hard work of the inner marriage (the *Coniunctio* or union of opposites) and escape to the potentially blissful state of the honeymoon?

Outcome

This is a work in progress as the client endeavours to hold the opposites in balance, sometimes succeeding, sometimes not. This is the path of Individuation, which rarely proceeds in a straight line but is beset with twists and turns, retreats and advances.

Shirley's Dream Series

> The meaning of my existence is that life has addressed a question to me. Or, conversely, I myself am a question which is addressed to the world, and I must communicate my answer, for otherwise I am dependent upon the world's answer.
> (Jung, 1983: 350)

Shirley is an experienced psychotherapist in her sixties and a dream group member.

Some time before this dream series Shirley had shared a dream in which she was a child. The dream ended with the dreamer hiding in a dark place and it was clear to the group that we needed to respect that place and not break into the defences around it.

This respect seemed to encourage the dreamer's unconscious

to reveal more of her inner world as, later on, over a six-month period, the following three dreams occurred, appearing to be linked as a series. They indicate a progression towards a greater awareness of the previously necessary but now obsolete strategies created in childhood to survive her experience.

All the dreams were worked with in the group.

Dream 1

I'm going up (climbing/crawling) a greensward with what looks like very bright green artificial grass. The mound is not very steep. At the top are my mother and sisters and in the distance is a pagoda. The sky is bright, but it is clouding over.

Then I'm in a block of newish flats on the seventh floor and go out on to a balcony. There seems to be no way down apart from two ladders from the balcony to the ground. One is straight in front of me, the other is to my left. Two men are at the bottom and could hold the ladder steady. I am really frightened. It is hard to look over the edge of the balcony, so I try to get back by the doors into the flat, which look out on to the balcony.

Context

Shirley had walked the Camino (a pilgrimage, a sacred journey) in the summer and had to crawl up cliffs on the way. She suffers from vertigo, where she can look up but not down. Just prior to the dream the dreamer was in the process of booking tickets to New Zealand for her nephew's wedding, but not wanting to go and be around her toxic family.

Group Dreamwork: Clarification and Amplification

Shirley is present age in the dream.

The mound: Shirley has put herself at the bottom of the pile and although the mound is not steep, she is crawling on hands and knees, which can be a position of supplication and/or it is what babies/toddlers do before they start walking.

What would it feel like to stand up straight and simply walk up?

The grass on the mound is bright (possibly drawing attention to itself) and artificial. Is the basis for Shirley's activity not real/valid and is it covering up something underneath it that she doesn't want to see?

Green is the colour of envy, but it is artificial so perhaps there is nothing to be envious of? However, Shirley's baby/toddler part believes there is and perceives her mother and sisters as having a relationship she is not part of, while she is left with an old fading memory (the figures look like a sepia photograph) of a feeling of 'togetherness' with them that she is trying to reach? Consciously, in waking life, the dreamer says, 'Why would I want to go there?' But unconsciously, a younger part wants to join them? The dream compensates for Shirley's waking attitude?

The pagoda: is a sacred space/tower in a foreign country.

(**History**: 30 years ago Shirley's marriage ended, with her feeling excited and liberated as she visited her sister in Thailand.[4] While there she challenged herself to climb up a pagoda, *knowing* she wouldn't feel OK but did it anyway.)

In the dream the pagoda could be symbolic of the challenges Shirley sets herself to overcome inner fears and what it means to metaphorically climb up then climb down afterwards? The pagoda might be a reminder of Shirley's tendency to climb too high for

---

4   While Shirley was away visiting her sister, she needed her mother to look after her own children. In the dream is the baby/toddler part of her trying to reach the mother and sister parts to look after her younger self? The dreamer was close to her sister at the time, but after the fairly recent and sudden death of one of her nephews at a young age, Shirley has found her sister's reaction very difficult. Is she trying to reconnect with something/ someone she once felt close to, perhaps the part of herself, like her nephew, that 'died' at a young age?

comfort and then find it difficult to get down from this place she has put herself in?

The pagoda could also show the sacred nature of the inner journey? The pagoda appears to symbolise a time of freedom in her life that is now distant and foreign, but at what cost?

The sky is bright but clouding over: this might show the dreamer that there is a degree of urgency for the inner work to take place in the bright light of consciousness before the unconscious clouds take over?

The block of flats: there is *no middle ground* between being on the mound and the block of flats. There is no transitional place between them, so it is either one position or the other. Shirley is struggling either to be with the mother/sisters (actual or parts of self) or she removes herself way out of reach.

(I felt suddenly very tired as I wrote that – a possible countertransference probably indicating that the process is unconsciously exhausting for Shirley.)

The block of flats is in an *urban* setting (likely to be a more head-based process) in contrast to the mound's rural setting (a more organic natural process), but where something artificial has been imposed, mirroring Shirley's internal world? Metaphorically the flats are a relatively *new* place for the dreamer to put herself?

Shirley climbs up (as with the mound) and puts herself 'above it all', where she is out of reach but isolated.

The balcony: a place to look out from and be seen (unlike Kenya, where Shirley spent her early years in a house with a screened-off balcony *so that she could remain safely unseen* while outside), but in the dream it is a terrifying place as there appears to be no way down from this position. She *knows* that in waking life it feels impossible to climb down from where she has put herself?

The flat: is on the seventh floor – this could be an indication of a link between Shirley at 7 years old and/or are there seven stories in her life? In the dream Shirley cannot turn back into relative safety but can only potentially get as far as the doors back into the flat. What does this mean for her, what formed as a survival strategy at age 7 that is still in place? It seems like going back the way she came is not an option? There could be a pun on 'flat', as in feeling down?

The ladders: there are two ladders, one directly in front of the balcony – a more direct way down? And one on the left that could lead back into the unconscious?

The ladders are like those Shirley climbs up in waking life 'to fix things', but having fixed them then has to make the frightening journey back down. They could also be symbolic of the dreamer's tendency to 'fix' things within the family – being seen as 'the one who can do it' – but it is then terrifying for her to metaphorically climb down from this position as she has no idea what the consequences might be.

Shirley seems to be more comfortable with looking up (the child position) than with looking down (the adult position).

The two men: these could be two animus figures (internal masculine aspects), possibly builders, who can help the dreamer by holding the means of descent steady so that she can 'fix things' (rebuild/let go of relationships?) climb down safely and ground herself.

General Observations

Perhaps the dream reflects what Shirley does metaphorically and unconsciously when she feels she needs to 'fix things' and/or 'rise above it' but she uses the 7 year-old's survival strategy to do it. The dreamer knows she is going up too high but feels she can't climb down and is therefore stuck in a terrifying place of dizzying height.

It felt important in the group that Shirley was not left stranded in the dream in a place she could not get down from. So we used a visualisation (see p. 136) where Shirley imagined herself allowing the animus figures to hold her steady, while she climbed down the ladder directly in front of her so that she could feel safe again on the ground.

It seems to me that the instinct and the archetype are irretrievably interwoven and here we have the possibility that Shirley's basic instinct and need to try and join her family on the mound is powerfully driven by archetypal patterning. For, if we do not belong, how do we survive? As children we find the necessary ways to try and find that belonging, but as adults this may become a hindrance to growing into our true selves. Could the dream be trying to bring this unconscious patterning and the way she tries to find its resolution to Shirley's attention?

In the interim before the next group meeting, Shirley felt the dreamwork had been powerful and transformative as unexpected changes in family relationships had taken place, leaving her with a sense of growing liberation. Shirley felt she had begun to stand up straight.

Dream 2

I am at the top of somewhere outside. It's flat with natural green grass under my feet. I'm on my own, then in a vehicle. I need to get down but there is no way down except for a rocky, narrow ravine with large boulders. Other people, men, are there now and I say, 'I'm going down.' They say, 'You can't', but I drive over the edge and over the dark boulders, which feels great, and I get to the bottom.

On waking, Shirley felt amazing.

Group Dreamwork: Clarification and Amplification

Shirley's strongest feeling in the dream is the conviction she can do it. She is present age and the vehicle is her four-wheel drive, showing that the dream is relevant to her current waking life.

Shirley's association to the car is 'you can go where you think you can't' and it represents her independence. In the dream she trusts that the car will get her down to where she wants/needs to go.

She does not recognise the setting (a new place in consciousness?) but it is noticeable that in contrast to the first dream the green grass is natural, which could indicate that a more organic inner process is taking place.

The bottom of the ravine is sandy and light, while the way down is dark and full of obstacles.

In the dream Shirley *knows* she can go down, but inner masculine aspects (animus figures) tell her she can't and they don't want her to go down there.

Here we could be looking at Kalsched's (1996) negative protective Self, where previously helpful inner figures try to prevent us from moving on as they work from outdated messages and belief systems and are terrified that change will threaten our survival.

Shirley's response in the dream is to say to them, 'I'm not going to be stuck where I am', as she cannot go any further and, apart from turning back, there is no other option but to go down.

The ravine: a place that is impossible to cross unless there is a bridge, or a way down is found. This feels important to Shirley, as she knows she has to 'get to the bottom of it'. There appears to be some collective masculine opposition to this plan.

We explored how it felt for the dreamer to make the descent. She was nervous because it looked steep and improbable with a massive boulder in the middle on the right.

This could show that there is something huge emerging from

the unconscious towards consciousness (the right-hand side), but the dreamer knows she is 'going to get over it'.

A boulder: is a rock that has grounded, having been broken off something bigger. It can block access or act as a stepping stone.

In the dream the boulders are *set* where they are. In Shirley's waking life she felt as if she was constantly trying to metaphorically 'get over' these boulders that had been there a long time.

Several puns emerge here in the evocative phrases Shirley uses. 'Get to the bottom of it', 'get over it' and 'boulder' spelled differently gives us 'bolder', possibly revealing that the dreamer is becoming bolder in her waking life.

Context

We looked at this towards the end of the dreamwork so that it had less influence on possible meanings. Shirley shared that since Dream 1, major changes were taking place within the family. A significant elderly relative was moving away and instead of Shirley being the person everyone expected to sort it out, other family members had, unusually, stepped in to help.

Shirley also shared that she was currently working with two clients with narcissistic mothers, which echoed the dreamer's experience of her own mother.

If This Was My Dream ...

We now opened up the dreamwork so that members of the group could make a statement prefaced with, 'If this was my dream':

'I would feel I didn't have to stay in a place where the only way down looks risky. I would get in the car, travel somewhere else and look forward to the journey ahead.'

(This would leave the dreamer still not 'getting to the bottom of it' and possibly shows a reluctance in the dreamworker's life to get to the bottom of something.)

'I would be really proud of myself that I had overcome my fears and found a way out.'

'It would feel like I'm finding my *own* way through something.' (Generalisation is often very helpful as a way of relating the dream to waking life.)

'For me the ravine suggests a birth passage, something I have to negotiate with a rocky descent that is scary but also exhilarating. It feels like giving birth to myself as a woman of my *own* making, not my mother's.'

'I'd be looking at how mountains are pushed up dramatically from underneath at times of potential upheaval.'

'I'd be thinking the boulders could be complexes that the Self, in its inner knowing, is telling me I can now find a way over.'

Shirley resonated with and felt affirmed by most of these observations. She felt her own narcissistic wounding had remained unseen and only became visible, like the boulders, when her early unconscious experiences of inner upheaval had emerged from the depths of her internal dreamworld at a time when they could be contained and worked through within the safety of the group.

The group felt that Shirley had grown up with a fear of triumphing over her beautiful mother, and in doing so had hidden her own inner beauty until she could safely give birth to who she really is.

Dream 3

I'm present age on my father-in-law's drive, made of tarmac/road planings. The house is a long way back from the road. It is very green around me, like a 1950's green. It is not natural greenery but like walls. My in-laws ask me, 'Where are you going and what are you going to do?' and criticise my plans for the bathroom as they do not want a change.

Then I'm in a magnificent bathroom with a huge sunken bath in a greenish colour. The bathroom has an area on the side for the loo, all a bit ridiculous according to the in-laws.

Then I've got to get somewhere and climb down some shelves with drawers with brass handles and tickets like an old-fashioned draper's shop. The drawers are pulled out, so I get a foothold. Below is a café with a lot of people chatting.

Then I'm at the top of a grassy slope with my partner beside me. It is the end of summer in open countryside. We come down the slope on a track in the middle. Opposite is a slope going up with a dead tree, massive and upright.

My old therapist (in her seventies) comes along, with three well-behaved Labradors off the lead with her. I have my dog with me and she is wearing her red collar. She is quite naughty, so she is on a lead.

The therapist says I should go up the slope where the dead tree is, but I choose to go along a path on the left with my partner and the dog.

There is a coal bunker in front of us. My dog pulls on the lead to fuss round the bunker and she won't be pulled away.

Shirley felt muddled after sharing this dream.

Group Dreamwork: Clarification and Amplification

Father-in-law: Shirley's relationship with him can be tricky.

As a possible inner animus figure this might be a masculine aspect of the dreamer that she finds difficult to relate to.

The drive: in waking life is a track but in the dream is made of tarmac/road planings. This is similar to the parking area in front of my house where the groups take place.

Drive is a possible pun as in the drive to do something, so could the dream indicate that the way to explore the dream is within the safety of the group?

The house: is a long way back from the road and appears to belong to Shirley's in-laws. Something is going on in a place that takes time to reach and does not belong to the dreamer?

Green: appears in every dream of this series (see 'Themes' at the end of this dreamwork). In this dream the colour reminds the dreamer of the 1950s when she was born, and appears not as natural greenery but as wall like structures around her.

Something in the psyche is 'walling the dreamer in' to her early life?

In-laws: are quite shadowy in the dream, possibly showing again that they could be aspects of Shirley that question her motives and actions, in this case her plans for the bathroom as they dislike change. This could be like having a permanent internalised judge and jury with the potential to maintain the status quo within the psyche, which stifles the process of Individuation.

The bathroom: is a place of cleansing. In the dream it is magnificent, a solid structure with expensive fixtures and fittings. The bath is huge, sunken and also green. Might this indicate there is a magnificent, solid inner structure in Shirley for the cleansing that needs to take place?

Who is the bath for – the internalised in-laws and/or the dreamer? Is there something that needs to be 'washed off', that is sunken but accessible within the unconscious?

In the dream Shirley walks around the outside of the bath, negotiating her way past the loo exposed in its own special area, which her in-laws experience as ridiculous.

A loo is a place to get rid of waste products, so might the dream figures need to let go/get rid of some psychic rubbish? The drawback could be that they can be seen doing it (i.e. exposed in the group)?

The shelves: are like those in an old fashioned draper's shop. The dreamer remembered such places from her childhood where she possibly 'bought into' something, perhaps chosen for her (judgements, belief systems, shame, internalised messages), that now she has once again to get down and over before she can arrive in a place that could nourish her – the café – but she doesn't seem to stay there.

The grassy slope: here Shirley is with her partner, perhaps showing that either her actual partner or an animus figure accompanies her. She is not alone on her journey into the inner world. Shirley is also at the *top* of the mound in this dream, unlike the first dream where she is at the bottom.

The end of summer: this could be symbolic of Shirley's life stage. Summer is over and she is entering the autumn of her life.

Open countryside: the dreamer is a 'country girl' who enjoys the outdoors and natural spaces. Open countryside might be inviting her to honour this part of her nature.

The slopes: first there is a slope to go down but this time it is not steep and there is a clear path in the middle so that Shirley and her companion can descend safely.

In opposition is another slope going up, where something huge has died but is still standing (again a generalisation that can be more helpful in relating the image to the dreamer's waking life).

The dead tree: Shirley knew that the tree had been dead a long time. The trunk is smooth as all the bark has peeled off. The tree has had its life, it's not sad but peaceful. The tree reminded the dreamer of her father and all the work she had done in therapy on her relationship with him.

The tree no longer holds life but is still part of Shirley's internal landscape?

My old therapist: is the person the dreamer did the work on her father with. It's not clear from the dreamwork whether the therapist arrives from the left (unconscious), the right (conscious) or comes down the slope featuring the dead tree. She tells Shirley she should go up the slope where the dead tree is.

The therapist could symbolise the introjected inner therapist in Shirley who tries to create therapeutic opportunities. Here she indicates there could be further work to do with Shirley's father, but the dreamer chooses to go to the *left* with her partner and dog.

The dogs: the therapist has three well-behaved Labradors who are off the lead, while Shirley has her actual dog in waking life, wearing her red collar and on the lead because she can be quite naughty.

There is a possibility that the three Labradors represent Shirley's three sisters who are instinctively 'compliant and well-behaved'. They can be trusted not to metaphorically run away off the lead, unlike Shirley, represented by her own dog, who is held under control.

The dreamer was the first born, followed by the siblings each with a two-year gap and Shirley felt she has always been unlike her siblings, with a different mindset. She described her dog as 'going her own way' with a tendency to be naughty. To continue with the analogy, Shirley's dream dog could represent her natural instinct to 'go her own way', but Shirley feels she should keep this part of herself on a lead in case she gets into trouble?

The red collar: this is the actual collar that is worn in waking life by Shirley's dog so that she can be more easily seen. Red is also the colour of warning and danger. Could the dreamer unconsciously feel that 'off the lead' she might be a danger to others or herself and therefore needs to be visible and under control?

The path to the left: here Shirley chooses to go further into the unconscious, along a clearly marked path.

The coal bunker: the dreamer remembered a coal bunker at her grandparents' house where she sometimes stayed as a child and another at her home when she was a single parent.

The bunkers contained a source of warmth but were also hard work. The first association, to Shirley's grandparents' house, might show there is something to explore about the time spent with them during her childhood. The second association might show that there is work to be done on the period of Shirley's life when she was a single parent.

Another meaning of bunker is a place to hide from danger.

The dog pulls on the lead to fuss round the bunker and won't be pulled away: does the dreamer's unconscious instinct to sniff round the past override the ego's need to move away from it?

Dream Themes

Green: the colour green appears in each dream. It is the colour of the natural world, one of the two colours of the heart chakra, often showing when change is happening in a person's life. It is the colour of envy. It was suggested by the group that perhaps a child part of Shirley was unconsciously envious of her sisters. This possibility was not easy for Shirley to take on board, but dreams often show us parts of ourselves we would rather not see. They take time to assimilate and transform. Dreamwork is not for the faint-hearted!

Up and down: there are 'ups and downs' in each dream, demonstrating Shirley's willingness to descend into and explore her unconscious dreamworld and to bring those unconscious contents up into greater conscious awareness. Perhaps also symbolising the 'ups and downs' of Shirley's waking life?

The buildings: none of the dream edifices or buildings belong to Shirley and it is not clear who does own them. Could they symbolise Shirley's belief that *she* should be the one who has to 'inhabit' other people's problems and try to sort them out?

These three dreams can be seen as a progressive series where Shirley's unconscious is taking her through some experiences from her past that are currently affecting her waking life. An inner journey through the vicissitudes of life? The dreamwork is encouraging these issues to arrive further into conscious awareness so that Shirley can move forward more freely.

Update

During the course of the dreamwork it was noticeable to Shirley and the group that she began to look and feel different and more liberated from old messages and belief systems about herself, and this has been maintained.

Tracy's 'Waking Dream'

Tracy came to see me many years ago while I was volunteering in the National Health Service. At that time there was no limit on the number of sessions allowed and I worked with her for 18 months. She was a small, thin woman in her late fifties and was difficult to hear as she often kept her head down and seemed to find communicating very challenging. Tracy eventually managed to say that she found it almost impossible to speak to anyone as she would experience a 'funny feeling in her body' and would be overcome by fear that they would 'get back at her'. I gently acknowledged her courage in coming to try and talk to me.

Tracy had experienced a life of hardship and loss and a recent redundancy had unleashed what she described as 'a monster in me [sic] mind trying to take me over' and she had asked for help from her GP who referred her to me. The redundancy had somehow triggered a recollection from childhood, which she eventually managed to share with me. She had been terrified by a group of boys who had waited round a corner to spring out at her. Despite telling her mother, who confronted one of the boy's parents, she was not believed and the story was discounted, leaving Tracy with an ever-present feeling that she 'had done suffering [sic] wrong'. She had grown up feeling isolated and different.

Two weeks after this disclosure Tracy arrived almost in tears. A few days earlier she had experienced a cold shivery feeling during the day and had gone to bed early feeling somewhat fearful. She was lying *awake* when she began to feel even colder and very frightened, so frightened that she could feel the hairs on her arms and the back of her neck rising. She felt a heavy weight on her neck, arms and legs as if she was being held down and said she experienced a pain 'down here', indicating her genitals. She was unable to move or speak. There seemed to be a shadowy figure of an older boy and a voice saying, 'don't say anything or we'll get you', and other children whispering in the background.

As Tracy told her 'dream' she began to shiver and cry, hardly able to get the words out. She was shaking and had goosebumps.

To work with this 'dream' seemed likely to distress Tracy unbearably, so I simply reflected the 'dream' back to her – 'during the day you felt cold …' and so on – confirming and affirming her experience.

The telling, experiencing, witnessing and confirmation of this 'dream' prompted Tracy to say suddenly, 'But that's what it's like I can't talk to no one, I'm frightened they'll get back at me and I dunno (sic) what I done wrong but it always feels like I done suffing [*sic*] wrong.'

Had Tracy felt some kind of premonitory somatic awareness during the day when she was feeling cold and fearful? Had the disclosure to me of her childhood trauma unlocked from her unconscious the actual events that had led to Tracy's fear of communication? Had she been waiting all her life for something to get her if she opened her mouth to tell her truth? It felt that somehow Tracy had actually relived her traumatic, terrifying experience.

Perhaps the earlier sessions of therapy had eased the top layer of Tracy's fear of communication, thus allowing the stored memory of what had really frightened and traumatised her as a child to emerge. She had been able to recall the incident of the boys hiding round the corner, but had blocked the probable *consequences* of telling her mother about it. It is not beyond possibility that as a result Tracy was attacked and sexually assaulted by the boys who initially frightened her. They 'got back at her' for speaking out and she had carried the memory in her body ever since, effectively terrifying her into virtual silence.

The 'dream' gave Tracy some insight into the 'monster in her mind' and through many months in therapy she realised that all her communications had been prefaced by this monster.

As our work came to a gradual close, Tracy returned to this

'dream', going through the experience again but this time calmly and saying at the end, 'I think those boys did suffing [*sic*] naughty to me, you know down here, that's why I feel so frightened when I need to speak to someone.' She paused and her voice rose angrily, 'I hate them for what they done to me,' she shouted.

Through the 'dream' Tracy had finally got in touch with her fear and her anger and had found her voice.

Was this a waking dream or a vivid flashback? Tracy described it to me as a dream and it had those qualities of shadowy figures, disembodied voices and the inability to move that we can sometimes experience in our dreams. I do not have a definitive answer, only that whatever it was allowed Tracy, for the first time in her adult life, to experience the freedom of speaking her truth.

Tabitha's Dreams

Tabitha is a client in her forties with a history of complex trauma affecting family members over a period of time. Some years before coming to therapy, perhaps searching for comfort and meaning, she had joined an evangelical church where she initially found help and safety. Unfortunately, Tabitha had then been subjected to the doctrines of hell fire and damnation that, in her vulnerable state, she believed.

Eventually Tabitha left this church finding it too demanding of her time and energy but also let down by what she experienced as the judgement and hypocrisy of some church members. However, she was still unconsciously 'bound' by fear that participating in anything, such as dreamwork – perceived to be the work of the Devil by this church – would result in her damnation.

After working for many months with the traumas in Tabitha's life and with the therapy and working alliance safely established, we started gently exploring her dreams.

Recently, a series of dreams began to show a real shift towards a more free and personal sense of her own spirituality, rather than the dogmatic and fear-based limitations she had experienced. Two of them are recounted in what follows:

Dream 1

I am present age but at my childhood home. There is a large bonfire in the garden. There are some other people there from the church I used to attend, and they start invading the bonfire party. They expect me to feed them. I am angry and try to get rid of them.

The dreamer wakes up feeling angry.

Clarification and Amplification

Present age: this tells us that the dream is relevant to her current waking life.

My childhood home: Tabitha had mostly fond memories of her home. It had been a place of safety but also challenge, where the dreamer received strong messages about the perceived place of women in the family within a patriarchal society. As an adult, Tabitha rebelled against this by trying to find her voice as an independent woman.

The bonfire: what might Tabitha be setting fire to? As a child 5th November had been a time of family fun and feasting for Tabitha. Historically, Guy Fawkes Night marks the occasion when someone tried to blow up the government – a symbol of authority and control. Perhaps in the dream that authority could be the church?

Fire is all consuming, burning away whatever we choose to stoke it with. It can be experienced as a ritual cleansing of no longer helpful inner contents or the torments of hell fire.

The church people: Tabitha does not recognise any of them, indicating they are most likely to be the indoctrinated authoritarian aspects of the dreamer who had congregated in her unconscious and were beginning to feel left out by her exploration of a different spirituality.

These aspects have not let go and are trying to invade Tabitha's newly found inner place of safety and enjoyment, perhaps to lure her back into their beliefs?

They expect me to feed them: the abandoned indoctrinated parts of the dreamer are demanding to still be symbolically 'fed' by Tabitha, perhaps through continued adherence to the introjected dogma, but she does *not* feed them.

I am angry and try to get rid of them: perhaps the dreamer is unconsciously more angry than she thought with the people from this church and their belief systems. She is trying to get rid of them, but they have been introjected and are still inhabiting her inner world.

Anger, both with herself and others, seems to be the predominate emotion, as Tabitha wakes up feeling enraged.

At the end of this dreamwork I suggested to Tabitha she could maybe find that independent voice and shout at the figures as loudly as she could. There would be no judgement or condemnation of what was expressed. She started off quite politely and quietly, but with encouragement built up to several shouts of 'F... off!' We could almost feel the relief from the previously unexpressed anger in the shadow.

Outcome

Tabitha is increasingly able to access and articulate her anger, but sometimes comes up against her introjected guilt about feelings of anger that are sinful and 'not allowed'.

Comments

Could the setting of her childhood home also be about the dreamer's anger with the figures of male supremacy in that home? Is it the child part of Tabitha that is caught in the authority of the masculine within her birth family, and later in the perceived authority of the church?

Tabitha is aware of her anger over many external issues of injustice, but I wonder if this overshadows a much earlier rage with the unjust suppression of the feminine within the household?

At our session one week later, Tabitha brought another dream that she had experienced during the night. It is not uncommon in dreamwork that the dreamer will have a significant dream the night before a session. It is as if the unconscious understands it is being listened to and that the dreamer will almost immediately have somewhere to safely unpack unconscious contents.

Dream 2

I am present age and inside somewhere I don't recognise. Outside the window I see a wonderful display of the Northern Lights. Then I am outside by a clear, shining, circular pool. I am grasped by a water wheel and then taken round the pool and immersed several times in the water. At first I am not keen on this, but then I find the water is warm and pleasant and I enjoy it. There is no one else in the dream.

Clarification and Amplification

Present age: again, this shows us the dream is relevant to Tabitha's current waking life.

Inside: Tabitha is in an unknown place within her psyche. There is inner work taking place but there is a window to the outside world. This could indicate movement between the unconscious and conscious parts of the dreamer.

The Northern Lights: are a natural, almost magical, beautiful phenomena that only appear when the sky is clear and conditions are absolutely right. In waking life Tabitha had only seen photos of them. Here in the dream they manifest in all their glory just for her (there is no one else in the dream). Seeing the Northern Lights encourages her to go outside, perhaps to feel closer to them.

The clear shining pool: this has echoes of a pool in a previous dream but here the water is outside and contained within boundaries. The water has an almost sacred quality and being circular may be a symbol of the Centre or Self.

The water wheel: is mechanical and usually subject to being switched on and off via human intervention. In the dream Tabitha appears to be grasped unexpectedly and almost automatically by the wheel and she has no choice but to be taken round the pool and immersed.

Immersion in the pool: initially Tabitha is slightly apprehensive but quickly finds that the actual experience is comforting and pleasant. She relaxes into it.

Tabitha could not think of any association to the pool or the wheel that resonated with her, but felt they might symbolise the new spirituality emerging from within her.

I used 'if this was my dream' and suggested that perhaps after the initial reluctance to being immersed in a different spirituality was overcome, Tabitha had found the courage to let go and trust the experience. Could her circumambulation of and immersion in the pool symbolise some kind of compelling baptism into the Centre, the Self, where she could enjoy a fuller more authentic spiritual experience within the pool of life?

Here the past could be cleansed and Tabitha could be reborn

into a new personal spirituality uncontaminated by the evangelical doctrines she had absorbed.

Outcome

Shortly after this last dream Tabitha felt a sudden need to go to a concert of some kind. The *only* tickets available at such short notice were to a choir singing a requiem in an ancient chapel. Despite feeling this might not be to her taste, the urge to listen to music was so powerful that she bought tickets and went along.

If there had been an alternative to the requiem Tabitha would have taken it, but there was not. What could have been at work here behind the scenes?

The dreamer found the music a very moving experience, as if the requiem (an honouring and saying goodbye to someone or perhaps symbolically some*thing* that has died) brought together the past, present and possibly future inner and outer worlds.

Here in this ancient place of worship Tabitha could experience her personal spiritual path without guilt and fear of being damned for her beliefs.

Christopher's Dream

> Many crises in our lives have a long unconscious history. We move toward them step by step, unaware of the dangers they are accumulating. But what we consciously fail to see is frequently perceived by our unconscious, which can pass the information on through dreams. Dreams may often warn us in this way.
> (Jung, 1990: 51)

This is a dream of a male client in his thirties, a high achiever still striving to be even more successful by holding down a stressful, exhausting, but rewarding job. Christopher's frequent travels abroad meant that our sessions were sporadic, so it was not easy to hold the therapeutic process.

The dreamer appeared to have difficulty both in accessing feelings and finding the language for them. Although his focus tended to be on the external world, we did occasionally work with a dream, albeit with some difficulty as Christopher relied on his left brain to give him answers. Eight months after starting therapy Christopher had the following dream.

Context

Christopher had just arrived home from a work assignment in Europe. He was feeling exhausted and stressed out.

Dream

I am sitting in the back seat of a vehicle being driven down the middle lane of a motorway by an unknown male figure. It feels like a foreign country. There is a sense that we are being chased by something. Other vehicles are either side of us.

I am holding a sort of rifle loaded with a large copper and silver bullet. A red and white lorry is travelling at the same speed some way in front of us. I am trying not to be seen as I aim the gun at the lorry. I pull the trigger and watch the bullet travelling in a straight line towards the lorry.

Up ahead I can see that the road bends round to the right and I know that the bullet must hit the lorry before it reaches the bend. The bullet goes into the lorry, which explodes in a ball of fire and veers off to the side of the motorway. We pass the burning lorry and look across at it, but I have no feeling about what I have just done.

I suddenly wake up, horrified by my action and feeling I must be a really bad person to do such a thing as I am not like that at all.

Dreamwork

The dreamer felt he was both in the dream and observing it, showing both subjective and objective parts of him were taking part. He is present age but cannot see what he is wearing.

He does not recognise the vehicle he is in or the male figure driving it and has no sense of connection with him.

Despite the feeling of being in a foreign country the vehicle is right-hand drive, while Christopher is sitting on the left on the back seat.

He is not on his own on the motorway as other drivers are taking the same road that has no exit points.

The feeling of being pursued by something felt familiar and currently present in his waking life.

The dreamer has no association to the gun or to the very large, unusual bullet, which is copper on the outside and silver in the middle.

It is a bright sunny day. The motorway is approaching a built-up area with modern buildings.

The articulated lorry looks a bit like a Tesco delivery vehicle, but the colours red and white have no personal significance for the dreamer.

The preparation of the gun and the firing of the bullet is calculated and deliberate.

The ball of fire feels like total destruction, but in the dream Christopher has no reaction to it.

Exploration and Ideas

The dream appears to relate to Christopher's current waking life as he is present age. There is nothing to indicate that there is a connection with his earlier life, as for example wearing clothes he had as a teenager or being in a vehicle that he previously owned.

The dreamer finds himself in unfamiliar territory, both in the vehicle, on the unknown motorway and the feeling he is in a foreign country. His dream maker may be taking him to a part of his inner world that he has not visited before? The feeling of being pursued could perhaps be the drive to succeed?

Christopher is being driven by an unknown masculine part of himself that may be coming into consciousness as this part is sitting on the right and is in control of the vehicle. The right often indicates something emerging into consciousness, but it could also mean that this part of the dreamer feels it is right to be driving himself (as in pushing himself) at speed along a road that is difficult to exit from. Therefore, it is possible that Christopher is being driven by the ego, who is in control of the vehicle the dreamer chooses to metaphorically travel in in waking life.

The part of Christopher sitting on the left at the back and preparing and firing the gun could be a shadow aspect of the dreamer, who is unconsciously the 'back-seat driver' behind his waking actions. This part is trying furtively to blast the lorry driver part of Christopher off the road, who is travelling in front of him on his predetermined way 'to deliver the goods'.

The lorry is articulated so this could be a pun on 'articulate', as in the lorry symbol is trying to communicate something to the dreamer he does not wish to hear.

The dreamer may have become unconsciously programmed in waking life to keep going and deliver the goods whatever the cost.

In the dream the shadow aspect of Christopher knows that this is such a serious situation that he must annihilate the lorry driver part, who is still determined to 'deliver the goods', before he 'goes round the bend' that is just ahead.

However, the dream ego is still driving Christopher along the road that many people take towards perceived achievement and success in the material world. In other words, Christopher could be heading for a potentially disastrous burnout/mental breakdown unless he slows down, stops driving himself and finds a way to get off the road?

It is interesting that on waking Christopher tells himself, 'I am not like that.' This shows how he may wish to deny shadow aspects of himself that do not fit with the way he consciously perceives himself.

> How can I be substantial if I fail to cast a shadow? I must have a dark side also if I am to be whole.
> (Jung 1985:40)

Through dreamwork unlived shadow aspects can be acknowledged and integrated, releasing energy to help us make conscious choices instead of reacting unconsciously and often inappropriately to external circumstances.

The dreamer seems to be unconsciously detached from what he is doing to himself?

Over the years I have worked with several male clients going for what one of them described as the 'rocket ride' – the relentless pressure and stress of keeping up, performing and providing, to accommodate the Western cultural goals of male success. This is often the road to disaster, physically and mentally, with burnout a common result of being unable to exit from the rat race and stop before something happens to enforce this.

I was very aware of the absence of any feminine aspect in the dream, and also of the potent sexual imagery, but Christopher did not wish to explore this.

Unfortunately, Christopher's work commitments eventually became so complicated by frequent absences from the UK that it was impossible to continue the therapy. This may have been an unconscious defence against working more deeply with his repressed, depressed and other unconscious processes.

I was left feeling anxious for Christopher's welfare, which may partly have been a countertransference to his own unconscious anxiety about continuing the 'rocket ride'.

Comments

This feels like a warning dream trying to show Christopher the struggle taking place in his internal world that, unless heeded, could materialise in the external world as illness or breakdown.

Outcome

In response to my asking Christopher's permission to use this dream, he shared that the 2020 COVID-19 pandemic had acted as a 'circuit breaker' to his frantic lifestyle and allowed him to reassess his priorities in a very helpful way. It seems that it had taken an external event beyond Christopher's control to bring about a change in his internal 'programme'.

Andrea's Repeated Cycle of Dreams

Andrea is a dream group member and an experienced psychotherapist in her sixties. Frequent calls on her time by family members needing support sometimes leave her stretched to almost beyond her limit.

The following two dreams repeat themselves in a nightly cycle, the first then the second, with the cycle recurring frequently over several nights. The dream cycle may be reflecting the situation in her waking life that she needs to attend to. This is emphasised by the repetition of the two dreams, one following the other, perhaps showing that there is some urgency to the need for resolution of the difficulties.

Group Dreamwork

Context

Andrea was in the process of clearing the loft in her house, getting out the accumulated rubbish in there, *some of which does not belong to the dreamer*. There are stairs into the loft. There are things she doesn't want that she'd like to get rid of, including boxes of old training course material that she previously thought 'might come in useful', but she finds she can't bring herself to throw them out.

This might be a physical manifestation of an inner process where the dreamer is unable to let go of emotional debris that no longer serves her or even belongs to her.

Dream 1

I am present age on the west coast of Scotland in the Great Glen near Fort William and Ben Nevis. I am sitting or standing by a long loch, which, despite a wind blowing, is quite still. I am looking out over the beautiful view. It is sunset. There is nothing on the loch and no one about, everything looks deserted and I am alone. Then I feel I am floating in the sky above it all and looking down at myself by the loch.

Andrea wakes up asking herself, 'do I belong in this place of wonder?'

Brief feeling reaction from the group: 'dissociated', 'peaceful', 'anxious', 'out of touch', 'alone', 'above it all', 'wonder'.

Notice how group members can have very different feeling reactions to the dream content. The feeling reaction is subjective not objective. The dreamer may resonate with some (even if initially this feeling about the dream was not conscious), but not with others. The latter might be based on the individual member's experience of something similar or the dreamer could unconsciously be resisting the concept.

Clarification and Amplification

The west coast of Scotland: is very familiar to the dreamer as a holiday place of 'getting away from it all' where she can relax and enjoy the beauty of her natural surroundings.

The Great Glen: was created by a massive tectonic collision opening up a giant crack to form a natural 80-mile long route, rich in lochs and rivers, through the highlands of Scotland.

Ben Nevis: the highest mountain in the UK where the weather can be suddenly unpredictable. Some people climb the mountain successfully, while others lose their lives attempting it.

The loch and the wind: the name of the loch was unknown to the dreamer. It was a place of beauty and mystery waiting to be explored. The water could relate to the state of Andrea's unconscious – is it unfathomable? There appears to be no desire to enter the water, only to sit or stand and look at it. Is the dreamer protecting herself or is she perhaps reluctant to disturb her unconscious material?

The dream maker could also be using a pun on 'loch', as in 'lock'. Is it possible that symbolically there is something locked up in the dreamer's internal world?

In waking life, does the dreamer appear outwardly calm and unruffled, no matter what is blowing around and within her?

The beautiful view: brings peace to the dreamer and could symbolise an internal space within her that she can retreat to in time of need.

The sunset: the time at the end of the day before night returns. In the outer world this might indicate getting older, the sunset of life. In the inner world it might indicate something coming to fruition, or the opposite with an almost conscious content sinking back into the night of the unconscious.

Alone and deserted: in the dream Andrea experienced this as peaceful and refreshing with no one and nothing else to worry about or feel responsible for.

Floating in the sky above it all: floating for the dreamer felt carefree, but she is also ungrounded. The sky is the canopy overarching the earth, it contains the life-giving sun with its warmth and radiance. Andrea felt that this was like looking at a sepia photograph of herself, perhaps something taken in the past that holds a memory of calmer times.

Floating can also be a way of dissociating from unpleasant experiences, a way of necessary escape and survival or a need to 'rise above' something.

The dream might also be using a metaphor to indicate there is a critical part of Andrea that *looks down on her* just sitting, not doing anything, 'only' dreaming by the side of the loch.

Do I belong in this place of wonder? engendered a question in the dreamer: 'Am I *entitled* or *allowed* to be here, as I seem to have removed myself from this place of beauty and can only look at it from above, not actually be in it or allow it to nourish me?'

Perhaps Andrea has allowed herself initially to partake of the beauty, but this creates an inner conflict about her entitlement to self-care?

Then there comes a rapid and complete change in Dream 2.

Dream 2

I think I am present age, in a tall house with windows. But it is dark and I can't see out. It is light enough inside, although there are no lights on. I am running up the stairs on the left between the floors because muddy, horrible flood waters are coming into the house. No one is there.

Everywhere upstairs is empty and bare, although I think there is furniture downstairs. The water is getting nearer and nearer, splashing up the stairs. I am scared and running out of puff. Then I'm in the water. I won't make it to the top and the flood water will get me.

After retelling the dream Andrea felt anxious.

Brief feeling reactions from the group: 'really frightened', 'chaotic', 'frightened and overwhelmed', 'disjointed and disrupted', 'drowning', 'can't get my breath'.

Clarification and Amplification

The house: Andrea does not recognise the house but it appears to have several storeys, which might be a pun on the number of stories that lie untold in the dreamer's unconscious. Perhaps the house symbolises the dreamer's current internal dwelling place that is unknown to her?

The windows: let light in and keep the cold out but the dreamer cannot see outside because it is dark, while there is just enough natural light inside the house to see what is going on, perhaps metaphorically in her internal world.

The stairs: are not recognised by the dreamer. Stairs are a means of moving from one floor (storey/story) to another, either up or down. They are on the left, which could show that Andrea's unconscious shadow aspects are trying to help her move into a greater self-awareness of where she is in her current waking life.

Running up the stairs: this felt like a desperate urgency to get away from what was threatening to engulf her, perhaps unconscious contents relentlessly pursuing her?

Muddy, horrible flood water: this reminded Andrea of a river bursting its banks. The water comes in at ground level, possibly indicating that the unconscious is in danger of being flooded by muddied unbearable contents that are no longer containable. The flood water rises inexorably and follows the dreamer up the stairs. She has no choice but to keep going upwards towards consciousness if she is not to be overwhelmed by unconscious contents.

No one is there: the dreamer recognised a familiar feeling of being on her own with everything, but in contrast to the first dream this feels frightening.

The upstairs is empty although the downstairs may have furniture in it: Andrea did not recognise any of the furniture that was being damaged by the flood water. Downstairs in a dream usually symbolises the unconscious or shadow part of ourselves. There are unrecognisable unconscious contents that are possibly in the shadow and/or introjected and do not belong to the dreamer?

The emptiness of the upstairs felt bleak *as if no one lived there*. Is there something being laid bare for the dreamer? Have shadow elements yet to arrive in and inhabit the conscious (upstairs) mind?

The flood water is splashing up the stairs: the dreamer had no association to this, but it felt menacing, like something chasing and trying to overtake her.

I am scared and running out of puff: Andrea resonated with this feeling in her waking life, where she felt anxious about the possibility she would become too exhausted to manage the demands and commitments that surrounded her. Is the dreamer running out of time and energy to engage with the necessary inner work?

I'm in the water, I won't make it to the top and the flood will get me: the dreamer was aware of feeling completely helpless, unable to change anything. Her greatest fear is about to be realised, she will drown on her own unless she can find a way out.

At this point we checked with Andrea that she felt back in the present time and sufficiently supported and safe to further explore the dream within the group, so we went round the room with 'If this was my dream …'

If This Was My Dream …

'I'd check out if the dreamer can swim.'

'I would turn round and face what is behind me.'

'I'd ask, what do I need to do to escape the flood water?'

'I'd want to keep my head above water.'

'I'd ask myself, do I want to be rescued?'

'I'd be looking at all the contrasts in these dreams and relating them to my waking life – allowed/not allowed, up/down, beauty/chaos, still/turbulent, dark/light, threatening/safe.'

'I'd be wondering if some massive inner tectonic collision has opened up a crack in my unconscious that shows me a natural path to follow.'

Working with this dream was not easy for the dreamer, who re-experienced the panic and horror of the dream situation. As a group we were aware of how careful we needed to be and this was invaluable in supporting and encouraging Andrea to stay in the dream.

It felt far too overwhelming for the dreamer to act out the dream within the group, either with Andrea herself or someone else taking her place while she directed the action. Instead, we focused on trying to help the dreamer to find some resolution to her dream predicament. Visualising the presence of the group to assist her so that she was not on her own and understanding that we could support and accompany her to find a way out seemed to help. At a later stage, when Andrea has more resources available, we might look at standing together while she faces the flood waters.

Observations

The dreams seem to have been triggered by Andrea's waking life activity of clearing out the loft, which is the room at the top of the house (metaphorically the conscious part of the psyche) that is often cluttered up with stuff that may or may not belong to us. The dreamer is trying to sort this out in her internal world before it exhausts and engulfs her?

The coursework is material the dreamer has already learned, but unconsciously she is not trusting her own knowing so is torn between holding on to it or letting it go?

These dreams came across to the group as an urgent wake-up call and warning to Andrea that unless she took notice of her exhausted state in waking life she could 'go under'.

Instead of simply observing the necessity for some self-care, she needed to actually engage with taking time out in places of natural beauty.

There is still self-regulation within the psyche, as although Ben Nevis is in the first dream, Andrea does not attempt to climb it or swim in the unfathomable depths of the loch.

In the second dream, if she could metaphorically turn on the stairs and face the reality of what is inexorably pursuing her she might make known the unknown and therefore feel less helpless, as she would know what she had unconsciously been trying to deal with.

Andrea's dreamworld appeared to be a reflection of her external world – a place full of opposites, contrasts and conflicts, yet with access to inner peace if only she could allow herself to go there.

Outcome

Unfortunately, Andrea's waking-life commitments increased unexpectedly and dramatically, which meant she was unable to attend the dream group for the time being. Might it be possible that an extremely powerful unconscious defence was put in place so we could not follow up on the dreams? If this was so, the group needed to honour and respect the dreamer's own process on her inner journey. In the end all we could do was offer emotional support as and when we could.

Update

After my request for feedback on her dreams Andrea responded that she had completely 'wiped' the second dream, but it came back to her as she reread it. Andrea has now returned to the group, but as we were in lockdown due to the COVID-19 2020 pandemic we were limited to a Zoom meeting. When we are allowed to meet again face to face Andrea has indicated that she might wish to 'face the flood', with the group supporting her.

Jennifer's Dream

Here are two dreams from a dream group member in her sixties, who offers counselling within a healthcare setting.

Context

Jennifer's mother, suffering from Alzheimer's for some years, had died 12 years ago. Her grandmother had also died from the disease. The family sometimes mock Jennifer if she has a memory lapse, saying, 'you're just like your mother.' Jennifer had begun to be troubled by the thought that this might be true. During the day before the dream she had worked as usual, but couldn't help out with established family commitments because of lockdown during the COVID-19 pandemic. This left space for other things in her life.

Dream 1

I am sitting next to my mother but then she blows up like a puff of smoke and disappears.

As the imagery is very powerful it would have been good to see how the dreamer felt, first sitting next to her mother and then how it felt when she blows up and disappears, but Jennifer wanted to work with the second dream.

Dream 2

I'm present age and am on the Tube [London Underground] and have with me a large, full, but not heavy travelling bag. I do not know where I am going but get off the train, leaving the bag behind. I go straight into a department store, which is part of the station. I see an old lady in her eighties with white hair, wearing a cream jacket and a blueish neck scarf.

An alarm bell rings [the dreamer thinks this might have been her actual bedside alarm clock going off]. Everyone remains calm and heads towards the escalators. I now know in the dream that I am at Oxford Circus where I take French lessons.

There are four escalators in pairs, with one going up on the left and the other going down on the right. The old lady goes up on the first left one and I take the next up one. A younger woman in her late forties wearing a blue coat and glasses is coming down on the far-right escalator next to me.

I realise I am not carrying anything, including my bum bag, so I have no money, no cards, etc. and I remember I left it at the station. I am not worried about it and head up the escalator feeling calm. I am alone and can see daylight ahead of me.

Jennifer's immediate feeling after sharing the dream was one of calm as she goes up into the light.

Group one-word feeling reactions: 'puzzled', 'hopeful', 'outside', 'curious', 'familiar', 'something escalating'.

Clarification and Amplification

The Tube: is underground, possibly symbolising the unconscious. The Tube travels on designated tracks in certain proscribed directions. Dreams of trains can show that someone is going somewhere, possibly on a trajectory laid down by someone else where they feel stuck and unable to change. The dreamer is on her way somewhere, but her destination is initially unknown.

I do not know where I am going: could this be the waking-life dilemma for Jennifer? She has no idea whether or not she will develop dementia like her mother and grandmother.

She then realises she is at Oxford Circus, a place where she learns a foreign language as she wants to communicate better with non-English-speaking family members. When the dreamer gets off the train of persistent unhelpful thoughts about dementia *she knows where she is*, but does Jennifer need to find another language to communicate with the part of her that is not going along with the old patterns of belief?

The bag: is a typical travelling bag but *it is not one of Jennifer's*. The bag is full but not heavy. What load is the dreamer unconsciously carrying that does not belong to her? She *leaves the bag behind*. The group felt this was really important, as it appears that at some unconscious level Jennifer deliberately leaves behind the baggage that is not hers *and then gets off the train and goes her own way travelling lightly without the baggage*.

One group member wondered whether the bag could be a

'ticking time bomb' (the possible onset of dementia?) that the dreamer has been carrying round with her, but in the dream just leaves this possibility behind?

The department store: the dreamer *has* to go through the store to get out of the station. A department store is a place that stores and sells everything for the person and the home. Jennifer enters the store on the ground floor, which might show unconscious contents about to emerge into consciousness and/or that she is relatively grounded.

Despite looking through some clothes, the dreamer is not persuaded to purchase anything. Something is being shown to the dreamer that she does not wish to 'buy into' and has not the means to do so anyway? This might be the family's attempt to clothe Jennifer in the ancestral patterns of dementia?

The old lady: reminds the dreamer of her husband's elderly aunt with dementia, who wears clothes identical to those in the dream. Jennifer's mother died in her eighties. In the dream Jennifer is puzzled by the old lady who is on her own, apparently independent, and wonders if she is alright.

As a possible aspect of Jennifer, the old lady may symbolise the dreamer's anxiety that as she herself ages she may be on her own and not alright, but the dream compensates this attitude by showing that the woman manages very well.

The younger woman: is the age the dreamer was *when her mother died*. Jennifer recognises the coat as one she had at this age and she also wore glasses.

She could be a younger aspect of the dreamer who still wants to shop in the store of negative possibilities. What is she hoping to find?

The escalators: are something the dreamer uses regularly. Escalators carry people up and down between destinations.

In the dream the dreamer and the old lady are going *up*, maybe symbolising current and older, possibly the 'wise old woman' aspects of Jennifer that are moving further up into consciousness and away from outdated belief systems.

The younger aspect of Jennifer is coming *down*, so perhaps this part *is* still unconsciously buying into the idea that she will develop Alzheimer's? She can then make her way to the station to get on the train of old belief systems and perhaps reclaim the baggage of ancestral patterns of dementia.

The alarm bell: actually goes off in waking life, but when the alarm sounded in the dream Jennifer felt no one panicked but calmly began to move away from whatever danger was threatening. However, the younger aspect ignores the warning and continues in old patterns of belief.

Group members came up with 'alarm bells going off' and 'that rings a bell', but the alarm is also something *that wakes the dreamer up*, perhaps symbolically jolting her into greater self-awareness of her inner process?

Leaving things behind: Jennifer is unconcerned that she's left the travelling bag that doesn't belong to her on the train, which will now have continued on its journey without her. She knows the bum bag that does belong to her is at the station, where 'it will either be there or it won't', it doesn't matter.

In waking life, being without her bum bag would be a major problem, but in the dream Jennifer appears to be relaxed that her means of buying (into) anything might not be available – possibly an unconscious compensation for her conscious attitude?

I am alone: to the dreamer this felt like independence and freedom from commitments.

I can see daylight ahead of me: something is beginning to consciously dawn on the dreamer concerning her anxiety about dementia? This felt hopeful.

At the end of the dreamwork Jennifer arrived at a place of sadness. The whole group felt it. In waking life, before the dream, she had been looking at her possible future following the maternal, ancestral pattern into dementia. The dreamer knows from her own experience within the family and from her work what this sad outcome would mean.

The group felt that the dream might be trying to show Jennifer that she is leaving behind the baggage that does not belong to her, the hold-all that possibly carries those ancestral patterns. They are not hers to own.

The bum bag is also left behind, but Jennifer knows where it is and is unconcerned. Some of the group also had experience of family members with dementia and felt that someone with this disease would then search desperately for something they thought was lost or that they would not remember they had lost it. The dreamer knows where she has left something important that does belong to her.

We summed up with the possibility that the younger aspect of Jennifer was intent on descending into the unconscious, holding on to the belief she would follow in the maternal ancestral pattern. She does this despite the alarm bell ringing to warn her not to go there. It might be helpful to explore this aspect further to arrive at a clearer understanding of why she persists in ignoring the warning. The present, older and wiser parts of the dreamer heed the warning and calmly ascend towards the light of consciousness, leaving it all behind.

Observations on Dream 1

Could this be a very direct way of showing Jennifer that although she is sitting next to her mother, *she* does not disappear in a puff of smoke but her fear of atavistically[5] inheriting her mother's dementia does? The second dream might then be elaborating on this?

Colin's Dream

Colin is the same dreamer who experienced the recurring dream mentioned earlier (see p. 52). This dream is both collective and personal.

During the first COVID-19 pandemic lockdown, March to June 2020, one dream group met online via Zoom, initially to check in with each other, then at a second meeting to work on a dream. The dynamics of Zoom were so different to our usual face-to-face group that we all felt the work might be more contained if we worked on a dream from someone outside the group.

The group work took place in June 2020. Information about the dreamer and the dream was emailed to the dream group a few days before we gathered on Zoom, as follows:

This is a dream of a male client in his mid forties who I have been working with for a number of years, weekly for several years, then gradually spaced out until he now has a session every six weeks. Colin is a prolific and insightful dreamer and dreamwork slowly became the main basis for our work.

Colin had the dream the week beginning 13th April 2020, while on furlough from his work.

I have Colin's written permission to share his dream with the group and I have agreed to give him feedback on it as appropriate.

---

5   Atavism – ancestral patterns manifesting in current waking life – sometimes present in therapy as the client feeling weighed down, as if they carry a burden, the weight of which seems to be out of proportion to their circumstances. Perhaps the patterns come down the generations and are repeating in the client who in 'waking up' recognises the pattern and works to break it so that its negative influence in the family is discontinued?

The dreamer came up with the title while recently emailing it to me some time after the dream.

The Pe(a)king Pandemic

At first, I am observing the dream. There is a large open-air restaurant with rows of rectangular tables arranged outside the front of an opening into a building from which multiple dishes of food are being served by Chinese people to groups of Caucasians – a mix of all ages and genders – there is a celebratory or festival feel, there is light and vibrantly coloured decorations.

A man receives a round bowl of food and in taking a spoonful starts to retch and is overwhelmed by the stench of what seems to be rotten flesh. He is told, 'No, no it is supposed to smell like that, but it tastes delicious, it is the dragon fruit.' [Colin remembered the name of the food after we worked on the dream – Colin does not order or partake of any food in the dream.]

There is a revolt among the diners and dishes are thrown to the floor and people are being physically sick.

The Chinese people become angry and aggressive. Reaching out from the restaurant they start physically grabbing and pulling people inside into what is a very cellular and stark building with many empty rooms that have cupboard-like compartments in their walls. People are being segregated and shackled by their ankles, children rounded up, men, women each sent to a different compartment. There is an angry violent feeling on both sides.

I am now in the dream. I am standing in a car park at the bottom of the restaurant, which is high above me in what now looks like a fortress. It has a grey stone structure, almost medieval, with no doors or roads leading to it.

I develop a superhuman power. I can fly as if jet propelled from my feet. I have an overwhelming need to rescue those trapped inside and make multiple journeys up and down, carrying those in need and working my way through the different cells. I am scared but somehow not concerned for my safety and seem not to face any resistance from the Chinese people.

I keep bringing the people back down to the car park and then I wake up. I feel exhausted. It felt like a very long and relentless dream that I could not wake myself from.

Group Dreamwork

The dream can be seen as emerging from the collective unconscious at a time of great threat to humanity from the 2020 COVID-19 pandemic. It can also be understood as a reflection of the dreamer's personal, unconscious internal world that, at the time of the pandemic, was surrounded by upheaval and uncertainty in his external world that had no connection with the pandemic.

This dream was shared initially with me towards the end of a therapy session, so the group work took place before a fuller personal exploration of it with the dreamer.

The dreamer is first an observer, then is an active participant in the dream.

Context

The dream took place around the week beginning 13th April 2020, approximately three weeks into the pandemic. The UK was in lockdown. The dreamer's sister had been talking of conspiracy theories.

Our usual practice is for the dreamer to share the dream without interruption from the group. On this occasion I reread the dream at the beginning of the meeting, and we then went round the group sharing a one-word reaction to the dream.

Reactions: 'uneasy', 'power', 'political', 'panic then hopeful', 'Nazism', 'Auschwitz', 'disbelief', 'wretched', 'dark', 'dead', 'powerless', 'transformation', 'survival', 'choice', 'rescue', 'reflection'.

Resonance: as the dreamer was not present during the group dreamwork, we could only monitor our individual resonances, emotional and somatic, as the dream unfolded.

Clarification and Amplification

Without the dreamer's personal responses to the dream content, we had to rely on our own connections to the dream material.

The Chinese people and Chinese restaurant: There are many differences between traditional Chinese culture and history and that of the UK. Chinese restaurants are popular in the UK, but we eat a westernised, adapted version of Chinese food. The restaurant appears to be a cover for what lies behind it. The restaurant is already prepared for entrapment/imprisonment.

Caucasian: a light or white-skinned member of the human race.

The tables: are set out in an orderly pattern and laid ready to serve food to the Caucasian customers, in deep contrast to the chaos that ensues. Rectangles can symbolise stability, but the tables are knocked over. Who or what has turned the tables on the Caucasians?

Lights and festive feel: something is being illuminated, but the festive feel is a cover for what is really going on. A big con?

All ages: the dream encompasses all the generations, different genders and is universal in its application. It could also show the different stages of the dreamer's life.

The round bowl: the circle is a symbol of wholeness. The whole has been given but contains indigestible and disgusting contents – shadow aspects of the collective and/or the personal?

Dragon fruit: in the UK dragon fruit is expensive, it is attractive to look at but has very little taste. It contains vitamin C, which boosts the immune system. Something is being served up by the Chinese people that *they* enjoy eating but that non-Chinese people might find disgusting. We have to eat what we are given or there are unpleasant consequences. Be careful what you ask for.

Expectations: are what we hope for. In the restaurant we would expect to be nourished and enjoy a social situation in pleasant surroundings. We would also expect to receive value for money and what we have ordered. We would expect to be given a choice.

Rotten flesh: something dead or dying, is it animal or human? Associations from the group included First World War trenches, barbed wire and death.

Being sick: something is indigestible, cannot be swallowed and is being rejected.

Protest: in waking life, news footage had been shown of Chinese people in Wuhan being dragged away by police and imprisoned in their homes. A Chinese whistle-blower doctor is killed.

Protest results in loss of freedom of movement and speech, people are rounded up like herds of animals, like Jews being taken to concentration camps in the Second World War.

Anger and violence: the Chinese take offence if their culture is seen as being judged and criticised. Here there is overreaction resulting in anger and violence on both sides. Everyone is angry and violent, a reaction to the pandemic that has been expressed by many people.

Shackles: imposition, loss of free movement, unable to run away, dependency.

Imprisonment: a total loss of freedom and autonomy. *Lockdown can be experienced as a state of imprisonment.*

The cells: prison, coffins, catacombs, mortuary, insect homes. Collectively we are all in little boxes. Cells of the body.

The car park: a holding space for a vehicle, a personal means of transport, while you leave to do something and return at some stage to continue on your way. Can be time restricted. A break in the journey.

Fortress: something built to withstand attack. The Chinese are fortified against attack. Once the dreamer takes an active part in the dream he sees the 'restaurant' for what it really is.

No doors or roads: there are entrances and exits to the restaurant but not to the fortress. There appears to be no way to get to or from this building.

Flying: not humanly possible unaided, needs superhuman power, take to the air, rise above everything.

The rescuer: the redeemer, the hero, the saviour, rescuing can come at a cost to the rescuer.

Symbolism: is both collective and individual in nature.

Contrasts and pairs of opposites are numerous as follows: observing/active; colourful/grey; open setting/dark, grim enclosed setting; outside/inside; Chinese/Caucasian; expectation/disappointment; smell/taste; nourishment/poison; order/chaos; caught/freed; unshackled/shackled; freedom/imprisonment both verbally and bodily; high/low; grounded/ungrounded; accessible/inaccessible; open/closed; separation/together; normal/abnormal; familiar/unfamiliar; fear/courage; human/superhuman; internal world/external world.

There appears to be a huge conflict taking place both in Colin's inner world and in the collective unconscious.

General Comments

The customers don't want what is being offered; the Chinese insist we partake of what they give us or there will be unpleasant consequences (e.g. Tibet, Hong Kong, Huawei, COVID-19).

China is courted by the West for its cheap labour and cheap goods but what price do we actually pay?

All criticism of the Chinese is attacked so there is no freedom of expression.

There seems to be an overreaction to everything.

People are so caught up in the experience of the pandemic that they are imprisoned by it.

The dreamer, as every aspect of the dream, is enacting the drama triangle – victim, perpetrator and rescuer.

What might be 'peaking' in the dreamer's personal life?

The dreamer knows he must do what he can to help but he has to first overcome his fears. In doing so he is given superhuman powers and resistance fades, but this takes its toll and he becomes exhausted. He is finding it difficult to 'wake up' from the personal and collective trauma.

Group Feedback at End of Dreamwork

'In the beginning I didn't want to join in and speak out, then I liked the universality of it, the differences and similarities, the good perspective of different reactions. It felt transformative. The journey, collective and personal continues. I feel energised.'

'I went from unease to feeling comfortable. I wanted to ask the dreamer for his personal connections and reactions. I struggle with injustice and need to keep in tune with *my* journey so I can help others in theirs.'

'I'm reflecting on the unacknowledged "foreign" parts of ourselves that tempt us in to their world but then imprison us.'

'I couldn't connect to the concentration camps. Our role is to listen and reflect, and recognise how hard it can be to wake ourselves from our collective and personal reality. The inner and outer work is relentless.'

'I believe the pandemic is offering us an unprecedented opportunity to connect to ourselves, each other and the world around us, to change the unsustainable way we live, not be "conned" into believing we are free and to understand what is really going on "behind the scenes" both personally and collectively.'

'In our lives my understanding is we undertake multiple journeys where sometimes we are observers and sometimes we actively participate. We need to recognise we cannot "rescue" everyone, as some will remain imprisoned within themselves – too fearful to change. So what do we choose to "partake" of and what do we choose to leave in order to conserve our energy?'

'I feel there is hope and inspiration in this dream that transformation personally and collectively can take place, as the dreamer "wakes up" in the end.'

'The inevitable is happening as we cannot sustain life as it is. If we each do our bit, however small, something can change. I feel hopeful.'

'This dream seems to encompass all the stages of human development. In the beginning it seems as though we are free, then we are imprisoned by our personal history and now collectively by the pandemic.'

'The only way through is to overcome our fears and find our own power to undertake the necessary work with ourselves and those we work with. That is how we will survive personally and collectively. Seemingly small offerings but immense when they all come together.'

'I'm feeling very reflective. This is an astounding collective dream. I'm asking myself, can *I* find the superhuman power to use for the common good. Can *I* take that responsibility?'

'But most of all what of our need to rescue those trapped inside *us*, in *our* internal world so that we can then free the *external* world?'

Further Observations

In the following weeks several newspaper headlines appeared underlining our collective fear of China:

Universities given tools to defend freedoms amid fears over China.
(*The Times*, 25 June 2020)

Staying free.
(*The Times*, 25 June 2020)

Serve motherland, Beijing tells students in Britain.
(*The Times*, 4 July 2020)

Britain is under attack from a meddling and bullying China.
(*The Times*, 4 July 2020)

Colin's Work on the Personal Implications of the Pe(a)king Pandemic Dream

Colin found the space to look at the dream in relation to his personal waking life several months after the dream. By this time the experiences of his outer life had become almost inseparable from the symbolic meaning of the dream images and it was clear that the dream held both collective and deeply personal significance. As previously stated, Colin is a very experienced dreamer and engaged with this dreamwork *entirely on his own.*

Context

Colin had been employed for many years in a prestigious organisation where he held a senior position. Financial difficulties in the organisation emerged and it eventually shut down. Almost immediately a similar organisation offered Colin (and a few of his colleagues) the opportunity to transfer their skills to them and, after much deliberation and with some misgivings based on prior knowledge of this organisation, he agreed.

Colin's Dreamwork

I feel trapped, having been lured in by the offer of something sweet, new and unfamiliar/exciting with a new job and the promise of things being amazing, etc.

Yet what once nourished me – pride in my work, the standards I upheld suddenly makes me feel ill. The reality is unpalatable and the joy and celebration of being reunited with colleagues – we've been lined up and fed the same story – turns into a feeling of being trapped, shackled to the corporate process and our individuality taken away.

The inside of the new organisation's building feels like the inside of the fortress in the dream, it's grey, lots of small rooms bursting with people who feel like they need to get out. Outside, in waking life, a banner proclaims the inviting credentials of the organisation but inside it is anything but what it claims to be.

So, in a sense it's a front, similar to the dream.

Now I've been left with what do I need to find in me to rescue myself and others from this situation? I need to be brave, fearless of the unknown and lift myself up and eventually out, back down to a grounded place of safety – the car park in the dream – which is a temporary place of transition in a journey.

If I could go back into the dream, I'd like to find the vehicles and move away from that place on a new road and in the light.

Outcome

So in waking life I've moved on from, 'I hate it, I don't know what to do, I'm trapped and out of control', to 'That's it, I'm done, I'm getting out.'

I'm putting work in to think what else I can do in a sphere completely unrelated to my previous occupation. I'm looking at my transferable skills, which may mean accepting a lower-paid, less certain job. But I am now willing to overcome the fears attached to former securities in an acknowledgement that it will free me from where I am now and give me space to find that vehicle for the next journey, the vehicle being me with a new headspace and set of options.

Comments

Perhaps Colin could expand on how some aspects of Self may have a tendency to be enticed into something outwardly exciting and different, but the unforeseen outcome can be imprisonment by shadow, 'foreign' parts of himself. However, the dream ego recognises this and is already unconsciously engaged in rescuing those parts. It may also be helpful for Colin to engage more fully with the aspect of him that *can* stand outside and observe his inner process in relation to external circumstances.

Sarah's Dream

This is a very different dream, by Sarah, a part-time receptionist in her forties at a complementary health practice. Some time ago she had completed two years of a counselling course and become interested in dreams, regularly noting her own dreams in a dream journal (see p. 132).

Helen, in her thirties, works as a human and equine practitioner in the same complementary health practice, but is not a personal friend of Sarah's. Helen is an experienced horsewoman and owns two horses, Star and Vienna. Helen is not a client or member of a dream group but has been known to me for several years. She is aware of my interest in dreams and told me about the dream shortly after it happened. I had never heard of Sarah before. Helen contacted Sarah to ask if she would email the dream to me so that I had the dream first-hand.

At the time of the dream, the first 2020 COVID-19 lockdown was in place and, although the practice was open, only half of the staff were present at any one time, so Helen had not seen or had any contact with Sarah or other staff for at least 10 days prior to the dream.

The dream occurred in the *early hours of one Saturday morning* in the summer of 2020. On Monday, two days later, when both Sarah and Helen were at work, Sarah asked Helen how Star was and Helen responded that she'd been very lame, was on box rest but also had had a badly upset stomach over the weekend.

Sarah looked astonished, saying she'd had a dream about Star early on Saturday morning, waking from it about 6 a.m. thinking, 'I should tell Helen about this', then wrote it down.

This is Sarah's dream as written down and told to Helen:

Space – dimly lit with no obvious light sources, smelt of horse/stable but no visual evidence. No walls, stable door, hay net, water source, etc.

No introduction to the dream, I was just there in the space. Did not feel like a physical presence. Could not clearly say if Star was standing or lying down but I felt a heaviness against me. I was aware of Helen crouching but could not say what she was doing. I did not feel Helen was aware of me, we did not seem to be openly communicating.

The line of communication began with Star telling me where the pain was – 'It's my stomach, the pain is so intense and I'm bloated.' The next part is a little blurred. I am unsure if this came now or later but it was definitely in the dream as I was speaking to Star. It was around Helen not knowing what was causing her pain – I said, 'Helen would know if you had colic.' Star replied quite forcibly, 'It's not colic, it's different.'

At this point there was a feeling in me that I had got it wrong. I had questioned and doubted her. I had made a mistake and a negativity came over me about how I felt. Yet I felt it was important to relay Star's message to Helen. 'Helen, Star is saying the pain is in her stomach.'

There did not seem to be anything unusual in this exchange with Helen, she did not seem surprised that I was relaying the message, nor did she respond or acknowledge me in any way.

During my communication with Star, I felt the presence of Vienna on my shoulder. Again, not a physical presence and it wasn't his whole body, it was his head and neck leaning over me. He was whittering and stressing about Star. There is nothing definite I can remember about what he was saying, it was a feeling. I kept reassuring him that Helen would look after her and all would be fine.

I woke with a start, not sure if something disturbed me, which is why I generally remember dreams in such detail. The dream felt so real I almost texted Helen to see if Star was OK, but decided to wait until I saw her at work on Monday.

Some History and Further Context

Star had been lame for a few days prior to this dream, but neither Helen nor the vet could ascertain the cause of the lameness and Helen was left wondering where the pain was coming from. Star was given pain relief and on the Thursday was put in a small area of the paddock she shares with Vienna.

On Friday Helen noticed that Star's droppings were very loose, probably as a result of eating some weeds that she would not usually eat when out in the larger paddock. The horse looked uncomfortable as she was not only very lame but now had an upset stomach, so she was put on box rest.

On Saturday morning the droppings were like liquid cowpats and Star was even more uncomfortable, but careful management ensured that by Monday her stomach upset had noticeably improved and then completely resolved in the next day or two. Also on the Saturday morning, between 5 a.m. and 6 a.m., the owner of the yard was woken by Vienna, who was out in the paddock, whinnying and thundering around the field.

One of Star's habits is to lean heavily against people and if Helen is treating her and doesn't get it right the horse will fidget and seems to get irritated, so Helen knows she has got it wrong. Vienna becomes quite vocally agitated if there is anything untoward with Star and one of his habits is to lean over Helen's neck and shoulder to see what is going on and he needs to be gently reassured.

The extraordinary thing is that prior to this dream *Sarah had never met either Star or Vienna* and had no idea that Star leans against people and gets upset if Helen doesn't get a treatment right. Neither did Sarah know that Vienna's reaction in her dream was an exact description of how he behaves if something is wrong with Star.

To reiterate, at the time of the dream Sarah had not been in touch with Helen or anyone else from the practice for 10 days and could not have known that Star was lame or had a very upset stomach.

On waking, Sarah knew that even if Helen dismissed the dream as nonsense it was important to tell her about it on the Monday when they would both be at work.

Helen was utterly amazed by the accuracy of Sarah's dream and neither of them could understand why it was Sarah who had this dream as, although she is fond of animals, she did not know the horses at all. The timing of the dream ties in with the yard owner hearing Vienna out in the field apparently disturbed by something.

Shortly after this dream Helen took Sarah out to meet the horses but there did not seem to be any significant reaction from them, although they were exactly as they had appeared to Sarah in the dream.

So, here is a dream unlike any other in this book, dreamed by someone with no close connection with the subjects of the dream apart from an occasional working relationship with Helen. The dream is not pre-cognitive as the events experienced in the dream had already happened.

How is it possible that this dream came to Sarah, why not Helen or someone else with a closer connection either to Helen or the horses? Could it be that Sarah, who as it turned out was an 'experienced' dreamer, picked up something from the collective unconscious because it was somehow 'known' that she would not dismiss it but pass it on to Helen? Could it have been to open a deeper layer of understanding and awareness in Helen?

Another fascinating aspect of this dream is that Sarah could actually *hear* the words spoken by Star in an apparently effortless communication between species, in a way that somehow both could understand.

This dream leaves many questions unanswered, underlining the often unfathomable nature of our dreamworld that patiently awaits our deeper knowledge and wisdom. Blaise Pascal offers another intriguing imponderable question that could be relevant here:

> No one is sure ... whether he is awake or asleep. Seeing that during sleep we believe that we are awake as firmly as we do when we *are* awake ... We spend half our life asleep, in which condition, as we ourselves admit, we have no idea of truth, whatever we may imagine, since all our perceptions are then illusory. Who knows therefore whether the other half of life, in which we believe ourselves awake, is not another dream, slightly different from the first, from which we awake when we suppose ourselves asleep.
> (Pascal, [1669] 1961: n.p.)

Finis

It is my understanding that at some unfathomable level we and all around us are not separate entities but each of us is interwoven with the other with a conscious or unconscious connection within the collective unconscious. Here the microcosm of our individual humanity becomes part of and has access to the macrocosm of the universe, itself encompassed within the Anima Mundi, the Soul of the World.

So, when asleep are we dreaming in a more subtle dimension where we are connected to one another in some extraordinary way, in contrast to our waking life where the barriers of consciousness and rationality get in the way of that connectedness?

I am not offering an answer, simply looking at the possibility that in working with our dreams we have the opportunity to truly be at one with each other and that could profoundly change the way we approach and live our lives, ultimately bringing about a healing of ourselves and our planet.

> If change in the world situation is ever to come about, it can only come through an increase in the number of concerned and committed individuals engaged in the awakening

and transformation of their *own* consciousness and giving expression to that transformation in some form of service to the world.
(Baring, 2013: 460, my emphasis)

I hope this book will help and encourage you to contribute to that change by working with dreams in a safe and accessible way so that you and those you may work with can become who you truly are and live the unique life that is true for you.

It was a dream that first encouraged me to pay attention to the dreamworld and try to 'wake up and write it down', but at the time I had no idea how life changing that would be and how long it would take to travel any distance along that path!

Dreamwork can be inspiring, but also very challenging. It is therefore wise to share your dreams with an experienced, compassionate dreamworker who will not 'tread on your dreams'.

Postscript

As the writing of this book came to a close, I had a dream:

I have been staying in a place of healing. It is time to leave and I feel I should offer something in return for my stay so I enter the chapel holding my gift, a new, unopened pack of five Paper Mate[6] pens. I place them in the round, gold collection plate, but as I do so they change into quite ornate offertory candles decorated with scrolls. I am astonished.

This dream could have several layers of meaning, but I will leave that for you to ponder … (Freudians might have a field day …)

A few days after this dream, one of the groups met on Zoom. As we were unable to meet in person due to the 2020 COVID-19 pandemic lockdown, members asked me to tune in to them and 'choose' their angel and dragon cards. I did this shortly before the session with my eyes closed, so I had no idea which card was being 'chosen', including for myself.

Both packs of cards are relatively new, replacing old ones, and there are several additional cards in each pack, some of which we are still discovering.

---

6   These pens are identical to those I have used in my 'scribblings' for this book. I had bought a new packet three days before the dream.

My angel card was 'celebration', with an apparently masculine angel doing a triumphant dance surrounded by heart balloons and either flowers or fireworks. I had not seen this card before and it felt very apt.

I was surprised as most other angel cards show angels in colourful robes, but this one was more masculine in appearance, wearing a white top and trousers, with black shoes and blue wings. I was reminded of the animus figure in the cow/bull dream that brought the 'beast' under control and wondered if somehow, in the course of writing the book, he had been recognised and worked with and was now celebrating!

Celebration

The whole group was stunned by my dragon card, and I can say no more but to place it here for you to see.

Reproduced by kind permission of Val Young oneheartweb.com

Within the Egg of Wealth
Lay all the many areas of your abundance.
All that has come in and been received
Within each part of your life.
At the Centre is the Source, the Golden Light
that has infused and inspired you.
From its centre, it creates connections to
Your wealth of Wisdoms and experiences
And the support you have been given.
When all these areas are lit up and bright,
When all is acknowledged in the Light,
The Egg becomes one pure inspiration of Life.
You are now ready for it to infuse
This world with its energy, Love and insights.
The Egg is forever generating more energy
And as it opens, you welcome the Gratitude,
Inspiration and prosperity flowing in.
This giving and receiving – the circular,
Spiralling, expanding energy generated
Is being shared with all in a loving flow.
The Egg is open and actively engaged -
And you get your wings to fly and
Soar with new inspirations.

Postscript

I will leave the very last word to the Big Friendly Giant:

> Dreams is very mystical things ... Human beans is not understanding them at all. Not even their brainiest professors is understanding them.
> (Dahl, 1984: 108)

Keeping a Dream Journal

Every dream is a source of information, and a means of self-regulation.
(Jung, 1985: 21)

It can be helpful to keep a dream journal beside your bed. If you wake up from a dream, try to write it down there and then as our dreams can be very elusive. We believe we will remember them in the morning but often we don't and the dream disappears back into the unconscious.

If you wake up in the morning and then remember a dream you had during the night, write it down immediately or at least go over it a few times in your mind before you get up and then write it down later.

In your journal note the date of the dream, anything that stayed in your mind or felt significant about that day and what your thoughts and feelings were when you settled down to sleep – the context.

On waking from a dream or in the morning note your immediate feelings.

You can work through the dream by using 'Some Ideas for Working with Dreams' (see p. 134), either on your own or, more effectively and safely, with an experienced dreamworker. Record your findings in the journal.

Over time you will realise from your journal how your dreams help you to discover unresolved issues in your life and the changes you may need to make to live your waking life more congruently.

Some Ideas For Working With Dreams

The following ideas incorporate elements of the work on dreams by Nigel Hamilton, C. G. Jung, Donald Kalsched, Strephon Kaplan-Williams and Christopher Sowton.

Dreamer and Dreamworker

The dream is a call from the unconscious to look at something more closely in waking and/or inner life.

Try not to intellectualise or theorise but be more aware of intuitive and somatic responses to the material being shared.

The Dreamer

Title: quickly, and without thinking about it, choose a title for your dream.

Note and share whether you are *in* the dream or *observing* it or *both*. This can help you to understand whether you are actively participating in whatever the unconscious is trying to show you, or you feel the need to be slightly removed from it for the time being, or that a part of you is more engaged than another part.

Present tense: relate your dream in the *present tense* (i.e. 'I *am* standing in a field'), as if the dream is happening now.

Relive: it can be helpful to close your eyes and 'relive' the dream as if you are still asleep and also to remember how you felt when you woke up then share this feeling.

Feelings: try to get into the *feelings* in the dream and, as you relate the dream, be aware of where in your body you experience these feelings. Note the strongest or most persistent *feeling* in the dream and share this at the end with the dreamworker, together with the feeling you had when originally remembering the dream as it may be different.

Context: then give a brief outline of the possible context of the dream (i.e. the date and what stayed in your mind at the end of the day prior to the dream), as there is often, but not always, a waking trigger for our dreams. If you can't remember then it will probably have been an unconscious trigger – a news headline, a passing remark, someone's expression, a fleeting memory – that consciously you have not noticed but your unconscious has.

The context can be shared either at the beginning or end of the dream. If shared at the outset it can offer clarity but also have the effect of colouring the dreamer's and the dreamworker's perception of what the dream is trying to reveal. If shared during or at the conclusion of the dreamwork it may affirm the dreamwork or offer fresh insights.

Reaction: as the dreamworker goes through your dream try to notice your reactions to the process, particularly where you feel a somatic resonance with something that might be said.

The Dreamworker(s)

Interruption: it is very important *not* to interrupt the dreamer during the telling of the dream.

Check in regularly as you work to see how the dreamer is feeling.

Reaction: as the dream is shared, notice/note if you can *your reactions*, but keep these to yourself for the moment. It can be helpful, though, especially in a group, to voice, *after the retelling*, one word to summarise your *feeling reaction* to the dream before the dreamwork begins. If you have any insights while the dream is being shared *keep these for later* (see 'If This Was My Dream', p. 142).

Resonance: as the dreamwork unfolds there may be times of resonance, often felt somatically in an 'Aha!' moment. The 'double resonance' is when both dreamer and dreamworker resonate with an insight (Sowton, 2013). This is usually a reliable indication that both have understood something at a meaningful level, a kind of 'truth' emerging from the dream.

It can happen that only the dreamworker feels the resonance. This can mean that the dreamworker has resonated with something in themselves or that the dreamer is defended against the insight, not wanting it to be what it appears to be. *Always* respect a defence/resistance, as the unconscious will often bring back the defence in another dream for the dreamer to reconsider.

If an impasse is reached (i.e. the dreamer has woken themselves up when confronted with some kind of threat), the dreamworker can help the dreamer to imagine being back in the dream – 'dream re-entry' (Kaplan-Williams, 1990: 23) – and going beyond the point where they woke up and look at how they might act differently.

For example, there is an 'ogre' waiting behind a door and the dreamer freezes or wakes themselves up. Explore what the dreamer might need to be able to go through the door (which can be an important symbol signifying a threshold that needs to be crossed in order to allow an inner process to take place). The need could, for instance, be a companion, a weapon, a discussion (what could the dreamer say to the 'ogre'?) or a befriending of the 'ogre' (who could symbolise an internal or external threat).

If this is too demanding for the dreamer, *it is important not to pursue it and respect the defence.*

Clarification and Amplification

Begin the process of clarification together with amplification.

Clarifying helps the dreamer to understand more fully the content, images and symbols in the dream.

Amplification serves to discover and expand the *dreamer's* associations to and *significance of these images, contents and symbols to them* and how they might relate to their waking life – 'as within so without'.

If the dreamer feels 'stuck' and unable to clarify or amplify an image or symbol, ask them to explain it to you as if you had no understanding of what the image or symbol is. This can help both dreamer and dreamworker to 'unlock' the image or symbol.

Clarification and amplification are sometimes used separately, but if time is limited they can effectively be worked with together.

Sequence: go through the whole dream – beginning, middle, end – following the *sequence* of events, as every part of the dream can be important, not just the apparently more dramatic parts.

Some Questions to Ask

Other questions may arise as you go through the dream – try and use your intuition.

After each question amplify the dreamer's answers and reactions to the question. As you work explore if there is a *personal* significance for the *dreamer* attached to the dream (e.g. age/

clothes/setting/people/animals/objects/actions, etc.), but always *keep within the dream content.*

Is there a *collective or archetypal* significance to any of the dream symbols? For example, traffic lights on red/amber/green indicating stop, get ready, go; a station as a place of arrival, departure, journey, greeting, farewell; giving birth/a baby could be something new arising in consciousness, while death/dying rarely indicates actual death but can mean the ending of, for example, a learned behaviour or a destructive part of self; a circle possibly a symbol of the Self or perhaps an indication of 'going round in circles'; a school/college/classroom is usually a place of learning; the sea, and its presentation, often indicates the state of the collective or personal unconscious in relation to the dream content.

A *collective* symbol can sometimes be triggered by something in the dreamer's *personal* life, and vice versa, so that there appears to be a connection between the two.

Important: *help the dreamer to relate their reactions to their current waking life.* Remember, the unconscious will often try to show us in the dream an insight into our attitude to our waking situation. Often this is *compensatory*, that is we are not consciously angry about something but our dream shows us being enraged – the unconscious and sometimes uncomfortable truth about our feelings!

How old is the dreamer in the dream? The dreamer could be present age or younger and, occasionally, older or ageless. This helps the dreamer to understand to what age/stage of their life the dream is trying to draw their attention to. They may remember or have a reaction to something connected to that age that is echoed in their life now.

What is the dreamer wearing? The dreamer may be present

age but wearing something they had when they were younger or belonged to someone else. This is usually an indication that there is something unresolved from the period when the clothes, which themselves could be significant, were worn or remembered that, again, is manifesting in the dreamer's current waking life.

Setting: what is the setting of the dream and does the dreamer recognise it or anything within the setting? For example,

Outside/Inside: is the dream set outside (towards the outer life) or inside (towards the inner world) or both? Is it rural (usually a more natural place in ourselves) or urban (usually more head/intellect based)?

Light or dark or both: light tends to indicate that something is almost in consciousness, while dark tends to mean something is still mostly unconscious. A dark room with light coming in from, for example, a window could show that some light of consciousness has come through to relatively unconscious contents. It can also be trying to illuminate/focus on a particular aspect of the dream.

Time of year, day and weather: think of the aspects of spring, summer, autumn and winter and how they might symbolise the dreamer's state of being or time of life.

Generally, the time of day is indicative of where the inner process is in relation to the dreamer's psyche – the morning can be the earlier part of life or something new coming into consciousness, the afternoon the midlife or the new content developing, the evening can be old age or something coming to fruition or perhaps beginning to retreat back into the unconscious (the night).

The weather is usually symbolically self-explanatory (e.g. calm, stormy, dry, wet, hot or cold) and might reflect the dreamer's state of mind, inner or outer circumstances.

People/objects/animals: does the dreamer recognise anyone or anything in the dream? Generally, recognisable people/objects/animals can be that actual person/object/animal, *or they can more usually be aspects of the dreamer represented by that person/object/animal* – animals often symbolise instinctual aspects of ourselves. Explore the characteristics of that person/object/animal to see how they might relate to the dreamer.

Shadowy figures usually symbolise the shadow – unconscious and/or unlived aspects of the dreamer that they do not like or want to own. Unlived aspects can, however, also represent a skill or our creativity that may have been underdeveloped or repressed as undesirable during childhood. This content then lies dormant until such time as it can be safely admitted into consciousness.

For example, the veiled woman can be an anima figure for a male dreamer, or groups of (often young and sometimes disreputable) young men can be animus figures for a female dreamer; an indistinct artist figure or craft tools could symbolise unlived creativity.

Authority figures (e.g. policemen, prison officers, teachers, parents) can appear sometimes, often trying to control the dreamer. These figures can symbolise aspects of Kalsched's (1996) negative protective Self who try to hold on to the status quo within the dreamer's psyche as their place in the internal order feels threatened by the dreamer's drive towards change and individuation.

How is the dreamer relating to the people/objects/animals? Are they active/passive/observing? Are there feelings attached to the relationship? The relationship may reflect the dreamer's waking experience.

It can be helpful, albeit very powerful, to encourage the dreamer to *become* the person, object, animal to experience how it might feel to acknowledge that part of oneself, and perhaps live it. Also, to vocalise something that is not said in the dream or stay with scary content and see what emerges.[7] As before, *always* respect the dreamer's defence if they do not wish to engage.

Direction: the dreamer may be going north or up (i.e. stairs/escalator/mountain), generally indicating something ascending more into consciousness; or south or down (i.e. downstairs/cellar/underground), generally meaning something is either still relatively unconscious or is being grounded.

Going west or to the right tends to indicate something coming into consciousness, the material world, mind dominating feeling or the masculine aspect. Going east or to the left can indicate a more conscious spiritual journey towards the inner world or conversely into the unconscious or moving towards the feminine aspect.

Colour: colour can have a collective and/or personal meaning. For example, red can be seen as danger/anger/a will to power/an invitation (the red-light district)/life blood; green can be something emerging as in spring/permission to go ahead/envy; yellow as the sun/jealousy.

Themes: themes may emerge in a single or series of dreams. They usually indicate that the dream is attempting to bring an ongoing, unresolved situation or state of being to the dreamer's attention. For example, interactions tend to follow the same way of relating; the

---

[7] Grounding: if any part of a dream is visualised or acted out it is important to ground the dreamer afterwards. The dreamworker talks the dreamer through the exercise. The dreamer places both feet on the floor, inhales deeply as if the breath is coming up from the ground and takes the in breath all the way up the body and out through the top of the head. Then the dreamer exhales, coming down through the body and back into the ground under their feet. Repeat this three times, ensuring the dreamer finishes with an out breath into the ground. Check that the dreamer feels secure and 'back in their body'. If not, repeat the exercise.

dreamer is passive or active; acting/reacting in a consistent manner (i.e. running away/standing firm); finding/losing something; courageous/scared; angry/sad; or perhaps similar symbols, settings, people or situations appear regularly.

Puns/metaphors: watch for the possibility of puns in the dream, for example a house with two storeys might be saying there are two stories connected with this house (often a metaphor for the Self); an unmade-up area of ground can indicate that something is true and *not made up*; a shopping mall could suggest the dreamer is *buying or not buying into something*. The unconscious can have a sense of humour!

If this was my dream: *briefly* share with the dreamer any 'wonderings' you might have about what the dream might be trying to show the dreamer.

For example, '*If this was my dream*, I'd be wondering about the bag I left behind at my parents' house'; 'I would be thinking about how I seem to be stuck between two people/objects/situations'; 'I'd be asking myself what I am *really* running away from'; 'I'd encourage myself to cross that river to see what is on the other side'; 'I'd be wondering about the animal I wouldn't let into the house'.

Finally: now the dream has been worked on, give the *dreamer* an opportunity to feed back their experience and possible meaning of their dream *to them*.

Important – always respect the dreamer's defences to any exploration of dream contents.

Remember: dreamwork is all about *exploration*, by using your imagination and intuition to try and understand more fully what the dream is trying to show the *dreamer* about their internal world and how it may be affecting their waking life or vice versa. Meaning and interpretation *may* emerge in the course of the dreamwork or in subsequent dreams, but can sometimes take a long time to be understood.

Above all, it is the *personal meaning of the dream content to the dreamer* that matters and not what the dreamworker thinks it *should* mean.

Dreams are a rich source of information and encouragement on our path towards Individuation, offering us a deeper understanding of who we truly are.

I must learn that the dregs of my thought, my dreams, are the speech of my soul. I must carry them in my heart, and go back and forth over them in my mind, like the words of the person dearest to me. Dreams are the guiding words of the soul.
(Jung, 2009: 232)

Glossary

active imagination – described by Jung (1971: para. 723n) as 'dreaming with open eyes', it involves concentration in a meditative state upon a mood, image or event, often a dream aspect, then allowing associated fantasies to develop. To be effective the result of these experiences needs to be engaged with and integrated into the psyche.

alchemy – the ancient wisdom involving the transmutation of unconscious contents into conscious awareness to form the gold of the true Self, the philosopher's stone. Jung's process of Individuation.

amplification – a way of gaining insight into the personal understanding of dream contents by associating to the images.

androgynous – a coming together and balancing of inner masculine and feminine energies.

anima, animus – the inner figure of a woman held by a man and the inner figure of a man held by a woman. The anima is usually a single, shadowy or veiled figure, while the animus is often represented by a group of younger men, sometimes badly behaved and occasionally dressed in black.

Glossary

Anima Mundi – the Soul of the World

archetype – the original 'blueprint' of instinctual human experience inherited by the psyche. Sometimes described as the energy around the universal experiences of life such as birth, death, mother, father, child, good and evil.

circumambulation – in the process of Individuation the act of circulating around the Centre or Self in a spiral, coming in and out at different levels and points in the never-ending journey towards the Self.

collective unconscious – that which contains all of humanity's archetypal unconscious psychic experience undifferentiated from the individual. The contents often appear in dreams, visions and active imagination personalised by the dreamer. Working on this inner world can bring the contents to greater conscious awareness.

compensation – a process usually shown in dreams of contradicting the conscious attitude to bring about balance within the psyche.

complex – a powerful and seemingly autonomous part of the psyche created from images and ideas experienced by someone that has been repressed into the unconscious. A constellated (activated) complex is marked by strong affect (the 'more than' reaction) and can cause difficult psychological disturbance.

Coniunctio – alchemically the union of the opposites within the psyche, often pictured as the sacred marriage between the inner masculine and feminine.

countertransference – the uninvited experiencing of the client's state of being by the therapist, particularly when the client is not consciously aware of their inner process. The countertransference can often be felt somatically by the therapist, who needs to have the capacity to differentiate between what is theirs and what belongs to the client.

dissociation – unconscious fragmentation within the personality seen as a splitting off into different autonomous parts of the psyche. Often emerges as a necessary survival mechanism during childhood trauma.

individuation – the process of becoming wholly oneself, the unique human being we were born to be, the recognition and integration of all we are. The journey towards the Self.

introjection – the taking in of aspects of another's influence that may not belong to the individual's own way of being.

narcissism – characterised by feelings of grandiosity and omnipotence that often disregards the needs of the other.

projection – the unconscious disowning of what feel to be unacceptable aspects of the personality and their placement into an external object or person. This is then related to as if it belongs there and not to the originator of the projection.

psychosis – an invasion of the psyche by unconscious contents over which the ego has no control.

rebirth – usually a long process of growth into a greater truth of a person's real Self.

the Self – an archetypal image that brings together the person's fullest potential and whole personality. The ultimate authority within the psyche.

Glossary

the Shadow – the dark, unconscious side of the psyche containing all a person does not wish to be. It appears in dreams as apparently undesirable aspects of Self or can be projected on to others. It can also represent the unconscious, unlived, often creative aspects of a person.

synchronicity – events that coincide in time and space but also have psychological meaning. These can be experienced as a meaningful connection between the spiritual and material worlds, the inner and the outer.

transcendent function – the symbolic bridge between consciousness and unconsciousness that can be experienced as a balancing between the opposites. Usually expressed through symbols and images that can then act as a safe container for powerful psychological experiences.

transference – the unconscious translation of a significant other in the client's life on to the therapist and then relating to the therapist as if they are that person. This can also take place the other way round.

Unus Mundus – the One World, the connection of all things, spiritual and material within the Anima Mundi.

Further definitions can be found in *A Critical Dictionary of Jungian Analysis*, listed in the recommended reading list.

Recommended Reading

Baring, Anne. 2013. *The Dream of the Cosmos*. Shaftesbury: Archive Publishing.

Bedi, Ashok Bedi and Jakala, Robert B. J. 2020. *In the Eye of the Storm*. Sacramento, CA: Mandorla Books.

Chodorow, Joan. 1997. *Jung on Active Imagination*. Princeton, NJ: Princeton University Press.

O'Donohue, John. 2004. *Divine Beauty*. New York: Bantam Books.

O'Donohue, John. 2007. *Benedictus*. New York: Bantam Books.

O'Donohue, John. 2015. *Walking in Wonder*. New York: Convergent.

Hall, James. 1934. *Jungian Dream Interpretation*. Toronto, ON: Inner City Books.

Hamilton, Nigel. 2014. *Awakening Through Dreams*. London: Karnac Books.

Johnson, Robert A. 1989. *Inner Work*. San Francisco, CA: HarperOne.

Jung, Carl Gustav. 1983. *Memories, Dreams, Reflections*. London: Flamingo.

Jung, Carl Gustav. 1984. *Modern Man in Search of a Soul*. London: Ark.

Jung, Carl Gustav. 1985. *Dreams*. London: Ark.

Jung, Carl Gustav. 1990. *Man and His Symbols*. London: Arkana.

Jung, Carl Gustav. 2009. *The Red Book*. New York: Norton.

Kaplan-Williams, Strephon. 1990. *The Elements of Dreamwork*. Boston, MA: Element Books.

Samuels, Andrew, Shorter, Bani and Plaut, Fred. 1986. *A Critical Dictionary of Jungian Analysis*. London: Routledge.

Sowton, Christopher. 2013. *The Dreamworking Manual*. Toronto, ON: Sowton.

Stein, Murray. 1998. *Jung's Map of the Soul*. Chicago: Open Court.

Stein, Murray. 2020. *Jung's Red Book for Our Time*. Ashville, NC: Chiron.

Stevens, Anthony. 1991. *Archetype, A Natural History of the Self*. London: Routledge

Ullman and Zimmerman. 1989. *Working with Dreams*. London: Crucible.

von Franz, Marie-Louise. 1980. *Alchemy*. Toronto, ON: Inner City Books.

References

Baring, Anne. 2013. *The Dream of the Cosmos*. Shaftesbury: Archive Publishing.

Carr, Michelle. 2017, August. 'Dream Deprived: A Modern Epidemic?' *Psychology Today*. www.psychologytoday.com/96/blog/dreamfactory/201708/dream-deprived-modern-epidemic.

Chodorow, J. 1997. *Jung on Active Imagination*. Princeton, NJ: Princeton Paperbacks.

Cooper, Jean C. 1978. *An Illustrated Encyclopaedia of Symbols*. London: Thames & Hudson.

Dahl, Roald. 1984. *The BFG*. Harmondsworth: Puffin Books.

Eliot, T. S. 1963. *The Collected Poems*. London: Faber & Faber.

Hamilton, Nigel. 2014. *Awakening Through Dreams*. London: Karnac.

Jung, Carl Gustav. [1935] 1977. *Analytical Psychology: Its Theory and Practice*. CW 18 (retitled): *The Tavistock Lectures*. Princeton, NJ: Princeton University Press.

Jung, Carl Gustav. 1953. *Psychology and Alchemy*. London: Routledge.

Jung, Carl Gustav. 1964a. *Civilisation in Transition*. CW 10. London: Routledge.

Jung, Carl Gustav. 1964b. *The Meaning of Psychology for Modern Man*. CW 10: *Civilisation in Transition*. London: Routledge.

Jung, Carl Gustav. 1964c. *The State of Psychotherapy Today*. CW 10: *Civilisation in Transition*. Princeton, NJ: Princeton University Press.

Jung, Carl Gustav. 1966a. *On the Psychology of the Unconscious*. CW 7: *Two Essays on Analytical Psychology*. Princeton, NJ: Princeton University Press.

Jung, Carl Gustav. 1966b. *The Practice of Psychotherapy*. CW 16. Princeton, NJ: Princeton University Press.

Jung, Carl Gustav. 1970a. *Civilisation in Transition*. CW 10. Princeton, NJ: Princeton University Press.

Jung, Carl Gustav. 1970b. *General Aspects of Dream Psychology*. CW 8: *The Structure and Dynamics of the Psyche*. Princeton, NJ: Princeton University Press.

Jung, Carl Gustav. 1971. *Psychological Types*. CW6. Princeton, NJ: Princeton University Press.

Jung, Carl Gustav. [1972] 1990. *On the Psychology of the Unconscious*. CW7: *Two Essays on Analytical Psychology*. Princeton, NJ: Princeton University Press.

Jung, Carl Gustav. 1977. *Approaching the Unconscious*. Revised and included in CW 18 as *Symbols and the Interpretation of Dreams*. Princeton, NJ: Princeton University Press.

Jung, Carl Gustav. 1981. *The Archetypes and the Collective Unconscious*. Princeton, NJ: Princeton University Press.

Jung. Carl Gustav. 1983. *Memories, Dreams, Reflections*. London: Flamingo.

Jung, Carl Gustav. 1985. *Modern Man in Search of a Soul*. London: Ark.

Jung, Carl Gustav. 1989a. *Psychology and Alchemy*. London: Routledge.

Jung, Carl Gustav. 1989b. *Psychology of the Transference*. London: Ark.

Jung, Carl Gustav (ed.) 1990. *Man and His Symbols*. London: Arkana.

Jung, Carl Gustav. 2009. *The Red Book*. London: Norton.

Kalsched, Donald. 1996. *The Inner World of Trauma: Defenses of the Personal Spirit*. London: Routledge.

Kaplan-Williams, Strephon. 1990. *The Elements of Dreamwork*. Shaftesbury: Element Books.

Morris, Henry, M. 2008, May. *The Seven Pillars of Wisdom*. Dallas, TX: Institute for Creation Research. www.icr.org/article/seven-pillars-wisdom.

O'Donohue, John. 2004. *Divine Beauty*. London: Bantam.

O'Donohue, John. 2007. *Benedictus: A Morning Offering*. London: Bantam.

O'Donohue, John. 2015. *Walking in Wonder*. New York: Convergent.

Pascal, Blaise. [1669] 1961. *Pensées*. Translated by J. Warrington. London: Everyman No. 874.

Sowton, Christopher. 2013. *The Dreamworking Manual*. Toronto, ON: Sowton.

Yeats, William Butler. 1994. *The Poems: The Wind Among the Reeds*. London: Everyman.